"Relying upon the growing body of evidence-based psychological treatments for PTSD, psychologist Sheela Raja assembles a treasure trove of useful exercises and skills for people committed to recovery. This workbook is an invaluable tool to accompany psychotherapy and will prove to be an outstanding complement to existing self-help manuals. Utilizing an integrated framework for promoting behavioral health, Raja's clinical skill and expertise resounds throughout the text. This is an important reference for patients and clinicians alike."

> —Terence M. Keane, PhD, director of National Center for PTSD in Boston, professor and assistant dean for research at Boston University School of Medicine

"Sheela Raja has produced an excellent resource for the many individuals suffering from emotional consequences of trauma that do not have access to, cannot afford, or prefer not to utilize traditional mental health services. Her book is long overdue in self-help literature. It is grounded in, and supported by, the best available research related to trauma treatment approaches. Readers can rest comfortably knowing that this is the relatively rare book written for trauma survivors that includes techniques proven to be invaluably helpful for countless others suffering from similar difficulties. They can be assured that exercises recommended in this book are bolstered by cutting-edge scientific research. *Overcoming Trauma and PTSD* is truly an invaluable resource—one that I will use often and recommend highly."

> —Matt J. Gray, PhD, director of clinical training and professor of psychology at the University of Wyoming

"Sheela Raja has written an accessible, clear, and compassionate book that successfully integrates important evidence-based techniques for the treatment of PTSD. She does an excellent job explaining techniques so that people can use them on their own, while also providing important guidance about when (and how) to seek professional help."

> —Holly K. Orcutt, PhD, professor of psychology at Northern Illinois University

OVERCOMING TRAUMA *and* PTSD

A WORKBOOK
INTEGRATING SKILLS *from*
ACT, DBT, *and* CBT

SHEELA RAJA, PhD

New Harbinger Publications, Inc.

Publisher's Note

This publication is designed to provide accurate and authoritative information in regard to the subject matter covered. It is sold with the understanding that the publisher is not engaged in rendering psychological, financial, legal, or other professional services. If expert assistance or counseling is needed, the services of a competent professional should be sought.

Distributed in Canada by Raincoast Books

Copyright © 2012 by Sheela Raja
New Harbinger Publications, Inc.
5674 Shattuck Avenue
Oakland, CA 94609
www.newharbinger.com

All Rights Reserved

Acquired by Tesilya Hanauer; Cover design by Amy Shoup;
Edited by Clancy Drake; Text design by Tracy Marie Carlson

Library of Congress Cataloging-in-Publication Data

Raja, Sheela.
  Overcoming trauma and PTSD : a workbook integrating skills from ACT, DBT, and CBT /
Sheela Raja ; foreword by Susan M. Orsillo.
      p. cm.
  Includes bibliographical references.
  ISBN 978-1-60882-286-7 (pbk. : alk. paper) -- ISBN 978-1-60882-287-4 (pdf e-book) --
ISBN 978-1-60882-288-1 (epub) 1. Post-traumatic stress disorder--Problems, exercises, etc.
2. Post-traumatic stress disorder--Treatment--Problems, exercises, etc. I. Title.
  RC552.P67R35 2012
  616.85'21--dc23
                                    2012027985

Printed in the United States of America

20 19

15 14 13 12

Dedication

For my wonderful husband: Your love, support, friendship, and intelligence continue to amaze and inspire me after all of these years.

For my amazing daughters: Your humor, love, and boundless enthusiasm give me hope and purpose every single day.

Contents

Part 3

Surviving and Thriving as You Look Ahead

Foreword

When we experience a traumatic event, such as physical or sexual assault, accident, disaster, or combat, our physical and emotional safety is threatened. We naturally respond with a range of reactions—numbness, confusion, fear, helplessness, horror, or disgust. Trauma can leave physical wounds to be healed, material losses to be replaced, and casualties to be grieved. For some, the emotional effects of trauma seem to diminish over time. The traumatic event is not forgotten, but the associated pain may be reduced. But for many others, the emotional and psychological toll of experiencing a traumatic event can continue to interfere with functioning, impair relationships, and erode overall quality of life. And it is not uncommon for those who continue to struggle with the emotional pain of trauma to feel helpless and alone.

If you are struggling with the consequences of experiencing a traumatic event, and you feel stuck, know that help is available. Having the strength and courage to reach out for help, by telling a friend or family member what you need, seeking professional services, or picking up this book, is the first step toward reclaiming your life. There is considerable reason for hope, even if you are feeling lost or overwhelmed.

In recent years, mental health researchers have made tremendous advances in the treatment of the psychological struggles that often result as a consequence of trauma exposure. For example, several approaches to treating post-traumatic stress disorder (PTSD), including cognitive behavioral therapy (CBT), have been demonstrated to be effective in reducing symptoms and restoring functioning. CBT is based on learning theory, and treatment from this perspective involves learning new ways of approaching and coping with painful thoughts and feelings. Techniques from dialectical behavior therapy (DBT) can be helpful for people struggling to regulate their emotional responses, improve their relationships, and maintain a sense of personal safety. Recently, approaches (such as acceptance and commitment therapy, or ACT) that aim to cultivate an accepting, compassionate, and mindful stance toward our internal experiences while also using traditional CBT techniques have shown considerable promise in decreasing avoidance and encouraging engagement in valued life activities.

The goal of this workbook is to offer you options for moving forward. Methods and techniques from all of these evidence-based approaches are brought together into one book as a way of allowing you to explore a variety of methods you might find helpful in your journey toward recovery.

Dr. Sheela Raja's considerable experience and expertise using evidence-based techniques, and her clinical wisdom acquired through years of work in this area, are apparent throughout this book. Her writing demonstrates the care and concern she has for those struggling with the consequences of trauma. She is warm and encouraging, and her respect for readers and their struggles is evident through her discussion of the pain and triumphs associated with PTSD and trauma. Dr. Raja has made a clear commitment to make evidence-based treatments accessible to the public. Although her discussion of treatments for PTSD is not exhaustive, she focuses on three approaches that hold considerable promise for people struggling with trauma-related problems. Finally, Dr. Raja acknowledges that you cannot heal in a vacuum. By emphasizing the importance of your physical health and your social support (from family, friends, and mental health professionals), she seeks to empower and educate you about your PTSD symptoms.

This workbook is aimed at encouraging you to consider different approaches, build bridges, and find a path that works for you. Although the hope is that the methods described will help to reduce or alleviate your PTSD symptoms, the book is written from the perspective that you are a whole person—with relationships and physical health that also need to be cared for. Too often, trauma leaves us feeling broken, with parts of our lives shattered. This book is aimed at integration, and it will be a valuable resource on the journey toward surviving and thriving after trauma.

—Susan M. Orsillo, PhD
    professor of psychology, Suffolk University
    coauthor, *The Mindful Way through Anxiety: Break Free from Chronic Worry and Reclaim Your Life*

Acknowledgments

I must first thank my husband for reading countless drafts of this manuscript. For decades, you have always been available to help me refine my ideas and edit my work. I am highly appreciative of my daughters, who have allowed their mommy to write without interruption. This book would not have been written without their cooperation and enthusiastic encouragement. I thank my parents, who taught me the value of education, science, and the life of the mind. You have constantly supported all of my academic endeavors, expecting nothing in return. I also thank my sister, who is my cheerleader on every new endeavor, including the writing of this book.

I have no words to express my indebtedness to the clients who have opened up their lives and their hearts to me as they struggle with PTSD. I carry your stories, your scars, and your triumphs with me every day that I do this work. Each of you has forever changed me.

I am indebted to many colleagues who helped in all phases of this work. Pam Weigartz listened to my initial book ideas and pointed me in the direction of New Harbinger. Eden Opsahl provided thoughtful suggestions on my early drafts. Matt Gray provided continual collegial support and spirited conversation on the ideas presented in this book. My research assistant, Chelsea Rajagopalan, provided help with editing and compiling references. I could not have produced this manuscript without her meticulous attention to detail and intelligence. I am grateful to my colleague Michelle Hoersch for working with me in the area of trauma-informed care. You have given me an amazing sense of purpose in my everyday work. My colleagues at the Women's Media Center, Jehmu Greene and Jamia Wilson, gave me the courage to think about writing and to have big dreams!

Tesilya Hanauer and the entire team at New Harbinger have been a delight to work with. You helped me shape my ideas and provided invaluable feedback throughout the writing process.

I have been blessed with many amazing professional mentors and teachers in my life. Thank you from the bottom of my heart: Cynthia Miller, Rebecca Campbell, Joseph Stokes, Stephanie Riger, David McKirnan, Robin Mermelstein, Cheryl Carmin, Kathryn Engel, Erica Sharkansky, Marie Caufield, Lisa Fisher, and Susan Orsillo.

My dear friends have encouraged me every step of the way. I could not have done this without you: Susan, Ben, Aashish, Kevin, Mona, and Eden. Finally, for all the brave and amazing women in my family who paved the way for girls to be educated, and for our spirits to soar in times of joy and adversity: Saroja, Saraswathi, Pavithra, and Sabiha. I learned from each of you.

Introduction

If you have picked up this book, you have probably lived through one or more traumatic experiences that continue to have a serious impact on your life. You are likely seeking relief from suffering, and from symptoms that may be affecting your ability to manage your emotions, form relationships, and fully participate in life. Dealing with a traumatic event can feel emotionally overwhelming, isolating, and frightening. You may be going to great lengths to avoid feeling anxious, which might in turn be limiting your ability to live a healthy, productive life.

You are not alone. It is important to understand that life-threatening, traumatic events are sadly common—but that surviving and thriving are possible. Exploring ways to deal with your symptoms is the first step in healing from trauma. This book is meant to help you in the journey of exploration and healing. You can use it on your own or in sessions with your therapist.

As a clinical psychologist trained in post-traumatic stress disorder (PTSD) and evidence-based methods, I think there is a lot of promise and a lot of hope in PTSD treatment right now—and that is why I decided to write this book. As a therapist and as a person I have heard hundreds of trauma stories from clients, friends, and family. And like most people, I've also had my own struggles with difficult experiences. Hearing about each of these traumatic experiences has touched me and changed me. I am amazed by people's capacity for resilience, growth, and change.

It is my intent to provide you with simple, approachable exercises that may help you with your symptoms. But I rely on your expertise to judge how these techniques fit with your routines, your personality, your strengths, and your life experiences. It's my hope that you will find a personalized combination of techniques and exercises that will not only reduce your symptoms but help you live a more fulfilling life.

Overview of the Book

This book is divided into three parts, each with several chapters.

- Part 1 will help you understand what traumatic events are, and will also give you an overview of common psychological and physical reactions to experiencing trauma.

- Part 2 goes into the specifics of how to manage the symptoms of post-traumatic stress disorder (PTSD). You do not have to have all of the symptoms of post-traumatic stress disorder to benefit from the exercises found here. This part of the book contains many exercises, which have been divided up by the type of symptoms you are experiencing (worksheet 6 in chapter 3 will be key in helping you decide which exercises are best for you). Your symptoms may include painful flashbacks and difficult memories about a traumatic event or events; a pattern of avoiding trauma-related situations and triggers; and a sense of being overwhelmed by or having difficulty with emotions and relationships.

- Part 3 discusses ways to get more professional help if you need it. It also explores ways to get more support and take care of your physical health, particularly after you have had some relief of your current symptoms.

What Are Traumatic Events and How Often Do They Happen?

If you have lived through any type of event that was sudden and life-threatening, then you may have lived through something traumatic. In addition, you may have witnessed or heard about something (from a friend or family member) that has affected your ability to function. Traumatic events include sexual assault, childhood abuse, domestic violence, elder abuse, homicide, street violence, combat, car accidents, fires, and natural disasters. Perhaps you have lived through a traumatic event yourself, or maybe you have seen it happen to someone else.

Sadly, traumatic events are not rare. When we look at surveys of the general population—that's normal, regular people walking around—we find a prevalence that is really shocking. Table 1, below, presents a lot of statistics about some of the major categories of trauma, gathered from several large studies and surveys. The point is not to bore you; the point is that if you've experienced something traumatic in your life, you are not alone.

Table 1: How Common Are Traumatic Events?

Traumatic Event	Prevalence	Source
Sexual assault as an adult	22 percent of women and 4 percent of men	Large telephone survey of US households (Elliott, Mok, and Briere 2004)
Childhood sexual abuse	28 percent of women and 16 percent of men	Nationwide study of patients in a large health maintenance organization (Felitti et al. 1998)
Physical abuse as a child	40 percent of women and 53 percent of men	Large telephone survey of US households (Thompson, Kingree, and Desai 2004)
Elder abuse	10 percent of people over age 60	Large telephone survey of US households (Acierno et al. 2010)
Domestic violence	22 percent of women and 7 percent of men	Large telephone surveys of US households (Tjaden and Thoennes 2000)
Combat (as a soldier or a civilian)	10 to 20 percent of men and 2 to 10 percent of women	Large-scale survey of the US population (Roberts et al. 2011)

Shame, Stigma, and the Cycle of Traumatic Events

Unfortunately, we know that a lot of shame and stigma go along with experiencing something traumatic. For example, fewer than half of all sexual assaults are reported to the police, so the rates of that type of trauma may be even higher than the public is aware of (Tjaden and Thoennes 1998). A good estimate is that one in four women and one in six men are abused as children, and again, that may be underreported. The reasons that people feel ashamed and confused after trauma are complex (as we'll see in chapter 1) but understanding the prevalence and association between various types of trauma can be the first step toward healing.

Sometimes, traumatic events do not happen in isolation—but rather, they overlap. For example, domestic violence is closely related to sexual assault. One fourth of women in the United States report violence by a current or former spouse or boyfriend, and this violence can be physical or sexual in nature. Almost three-fourths of women who are sexually assaulted after the age of eighteen are victimized by husbands (current or former), boyfriends, dates, or other intimate partners (Tjaden and Thoennes 1998). In another example of overlap, experiencing combat and warfare may also place people at risk for sexual assault. Between 10 and 20 percent of men and 2 to 10 percent of women in the United States have been exposed to combat, whether as soldiers or civilians. These people have either been deployed to a war zone or immigrated from a country where they were exposed to warfare. There is more and more information coming out about the levels of sexual assault in the military, as well as in war-torn countries (Hynes and Cordozo 2000; Skinner et al. 2000). Although we don't talk about traumatic events much in common conversation, it's important to remember that many, many people have lived through these types of experiences. Sometimes it helps a lot to know that you are not the only one who has experienced trauma—that you are not alone.

You may have experienced more than one traumatic event in your life. All of the exercises in this book can apply to you too. People who have experienced more than one traumatic event sometimes have the most difficult time coping, and often blame themselves. But it is not your fault. Specifically, there seems to be a relationship between experiencing traumatic events as a child or adolescent and experiencing other traumas as an adult. When you experience stressful events early in your life, you may have difficulty trusting other people, and you may have no models of what a "good" relationship should look like. You may have felt lonely and isolated, which may have put you at risk for other types of traumatic events. Once you experienced the traumatic event or events, you may have turned to unhealthy ways of coping with your feelings (as we'll discuss in chapter 2), including alcohol, drug use, and risky sexual behavior. Although this way of coping might help you in the short term, it doesn't work well in the long term. It may make you more vulnerable to future trauma, setting up a very scary cycle. But you can break this cycle with some of the techniques in this book (see worksheet 5 to assess whether you may need professional help overcoming the effects of trauma). Figure 1 illustrates the complicated relationship between early traumatic events, feelings, ways of coping, and adult trauma.

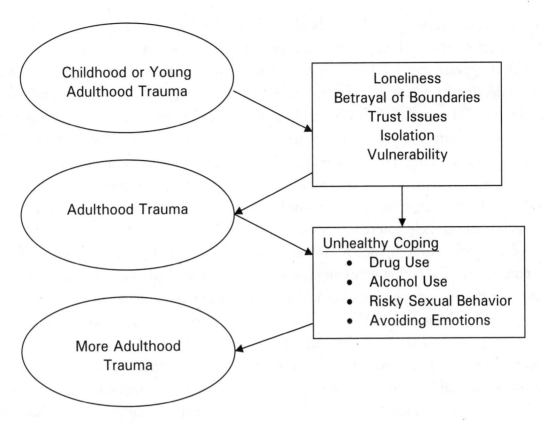

Figure 1: The Cycle of Traumatic Events

Techniques and Therapies in This Book

There have been a lot of advances in the treatment of PTSD and trauma in recent decades. This book brings three therapies for PTSD together in one accessible workbook. These treatments are cognitive behavioral therapy (CBT), dialectical behavior therapy (DBT), and acceptance and commitment therapy (ACT). The treatments are either evidence-based or are based on promising emerging evidence. *Evidence-based* simply means that the therapy has been looked at in many studies and found to be effective. To meet the standard of evidence, these studies usually include a group of clients assigned to the therapy being studied, a group assigned to supportive talk therapy (which is not necessarily focused on the specific symptoms), and a group assigned to a waiting list. If the clients who receive the therapy being studied have fewer symptoms and maintain their gains longer than the other groups, a therapy is said to be evidence-based. Cognitive behavioral therapy (CBT) has been looked at in this way and found to be helpful in reducing the symptoms of PTSD. The two other treatments we'll use in this book, dialectical behavior therapy (DBT) and acceptance and commitment therapy (ACT), appear to hold strong promise for certain aspects of PTSD. It appears that DBT is a promising adjunctive treatment for PTSD, particularly if you are dealing with thoughts of hurting yourself or others, or struggling to handle impulsive behaviors (Harned et al. 2010). And ACT has been very effective in helping people who are experiencing large amounts of anxiety (Eifert and Forsyth 2005), and anxiety is a key component of PTSD. This book will help you understand the common elements across these therapies and will suggest how you might use specific techniques from each therapy for different PTSD symptoms. In other words, this book gives you access to more evidence-based techniques to help you reduce your symptoms and live the life you want.

Cognitive behavioral therapy (CBT) has been used for PTSD for over thirty years. The basic premise of CBT is that changing the way we think and the way we behave can help us function better and deal with difficulties. Thus CBT tends to focus on your current functioning. At a basic level, CBT is all about looking at our thoughts and our behaviors—and changing them if needed. One aspect of CBT for PTSD is called *exposure therapy*. Exposure therapy isn't something frightening or scary—although it can sound very overwhelming. It is simply about "exposing" yourself to your trauma memories in small, manageable steps. You remain in control of the process. Remember, many people spend a great deal of time and effort trying to avoid memories and feelings associated with traumatic events, and this really has an impact on the quality of their lives. Learning to deal with memories allows people to fully participate in life experiences and pursue activities that they value. Before you can start exposure, you've got to make sure you know how to cope with those memories. So you will first learn how to cope if you begin to feel emotionally overwhelmed. There are several exercises that will help you learn these techniques.

Dialectical behavior therapy can also help people who have undergone traumatic events—particularly early in life. It has a very nonjudgmental approach to helping people understand their problems. For example, having certain *invalidating experiences* when you are young can cause you to constantly question your own judgment. As an adult, you may also have difficulty making decisions, trusting others, managing your feelings, and forming close relationships. What is an example of an invalidating experience? Let's say a child is hungry and says, "Mommy, I want to eat." The normal response is that the mother feeds the child. However, if a mother repeatedly denies the validity of the child's experience by saying, "No, you are not hungry," that child learns to distrust her own inner voice, her own physiology, and her own emotions. Dialectical behavior therapy skills are focused on developing an awareness of what is happening around you (mindfulness), learning how to form better relationships with people, and improving your ability to manage difficult emotions. You do not need to have experienced childhood trauma to benefit from DBT techniques.

Acceptance and commitment therapy is a newer treatment that has been applied to anxiety and PTSD. It has a focus on accepting your thoughts and emotions (even negative ones) rather than trying to change them. Many CBT techniques involve changing your thoughts, and ACT can help you accept the ones you can't change. Acceptance and commitment therapy techniques can also help you identify your own values and make a commitment to working toward them.

Each one of these treatments can help you with certain PTSD symptoms (chapter 3 contains more information about which therapies are useful for which symptoms). Recently, there has been a great interest in combining and integrating these treatments (Barlow and Durand 2011). Overall, the three therapies have a lot of elements in common. For example, all three emphasize facing difficult circumstances in small, manageable steps, rather than avoiding thoughts, feelings, and situations. Also, all the treatments will help you to identify your emotions, understand situations that might trigger negative emotions, and help you to plan for healthy ways to cope (Hoffman, Sayer, and Fang 2010). The goal of this workbook is to give you access to a wider array of effective and highly promising treatment techniques for PTSD. In chapter 3, worksheet 6 will allow you to find suggested exercises based on your symptom profile. These techniques come from all three of these evidence-based therapies.

How to Use This Book

You do not need to be diagnosed with post-traumatic stress disorder to benefit from this book. If you have experienced any type of traumatic event that is affecting your ability to function—that is, to go to work or school, form relationships, or enjoy your life fully—you may want to consider these exercises. This book will ask you be active! This book is also based on a belief in your ability to make changes in your life. That is, you should be willing to try various exercises and see how they fit for you. See how you can tailor things to make them work for your life. I am continually amazed at the way clients find ways to personalize these techniques and make them their own. If you have a therapist, you can work together to choose the exercises that might be right for you.

Part 1

What Is Trauma and How Can It Affect Your Life?

Chapter 1

How People Respond
to Traumatic Events

People are not robots—they have complicated thoughts, feelings, and emotions. That's why it is perfectly normal to react to traumatic events; it makes us human. Most of us start out as loving, trusting people. Trauma interferes with some of our basic assumptions about the world. For example, many people believe on some level that the world is predictable, or that bad things don't happen to good people. The fact that trauma changes your basic beliefs about the world is why it is so difficult to process on your own.

What Is Trauma?

In common conversation, people sometimes use the word "traumatic" interchangeably with "stressful." If you've lived through a traumatic event, you know trauma and stress are not the same thing. Everyday hassles (for example, a long commute) and even enduring difficulties (for example, dealing with unemployment) can be stressful. The difference is that traumatic events are life-threatening. With a traumatic event:

- You experience or witness a situation that involves threat of actual death or serious injury.

- You experience or witness a situation where your physical well-being—or someone else's—is seriously threatened.

- You react to what you've experienced or witnessed with fear, helplessness, or horror.

Based on this list, you can see why things like combat, being physically or sexually assaulted, or living through a natural disaster or car accident are types of traumatic events. They involve a serious threat to your life (or the lives of those around you) and your physical safety.

In worksheet 1, you will take a look at your potentially traumatic life experiences. A number of the more common traumatic events are listed down the left side of the page. There is also room near the bottom to fill in a traumatic event (or events) that isn't on the list—just remember the criteria of a serious physical threat to life and safety (either yours or someone else's). The point of this exercise is not to overwhelm you. You do not need to go into great detail about any of these events, you simply need to see if any of them have happened to you. It takes a great deal of courage to start looking at these events, and it is the first step toward healing.

Worksheet 1: Have I Experienced a Traumatic Event?

Purpose: To see if you have experienced traumatic events, and if so, what they were.

Instructions: For each of these categories of traumatic events, write down whether you experienced or witnessed it and, if so, whether your life or safety, or someone else's life or safety, was in danger. Describe briefly (in a few words or a sentence) how you reacted to the event. Use more paper if you need to.

Difficult Experience	Experienced or Witnessed It?	Was My Life (or Someone Else's Life) in Danger or Was My Safety (or Someone Else's) Threatened?	How I Reacted
Example: Sexual assault (as an adult)	*Happened to me last year*	Yes	*I felt completely helpless, frightened, and numb—I was shocked that this could happen to me.*
Fire, flood, or other natural disaster			
Accident (for example, car accident or explosion)			
Unwanted sexual contact before the age of eighteen (childhood sexual abuse)			

Unwanted sexual contact as an adult			
Physical assault or threat of assault by someone you know (for example, domestic violence)			
Physical assault or threat of assault by a stranger or in your community (for example, mugging, stabbing, or shooting)			
Exposure to combat as a soldier or civilian			
Captivity, imprisonment, or torture			
Sudden, unexpected death of a loved one			
Other:			

What Is PTSD?

Post-traumatic stress disorder (PTSD) is a common reaction to experiencing something traumatic. To have a diagnosis of PTSD, you need to have been exposed to a traumatic event that involved death, threat of death, injury, or threat to the physical safety of yourself or someone else. Your reaction to this event usually involves intense fear, helplessness, or horror. In addition, after the trauma, you experience one or more of these other types of symptoms: re-experiencing, avoidance, or feeling constantly anxious or on edge.

Re-experiencing

There are various ways that a traumatic event can be re-experienced. People with PTSD often experience bad dreams about the event; may have distressing memories of the trauma; and may have times they feel the trauma is actually happening all over again. In addition, you may feel very emotionally or physically distressed when you are re-experiencing traumatic events. For example, your heart might start racing, you might start crying uncontrollably, or you might feel highly anxious.

CASE EXAMPLE

Don is a twenty-five-year-old veteran who served in the US military as a marine. He was deployed three times to Iraq and Afghanistan over the course of twenty-eight months. Don and his unit experienced hostile fire on numerous occasions. Don says the most distressing incident took place when his good friend and fellow marine was killed in a sniper attack. They were in the same vehicle on a street in Iraq. His friend died before they could get him medical attention, and Don held him during the last moments of his life. Since returning home, Don has had trouble sleeping because of nightmares, and he is very reactive to loud noises and people walking behind him. When Don watches television, any violent images can trigger a flashback. Once when he was watching the local news, he saw some footage of a car accident. It brought back vivid memories of holding his injured friend. Don said he was shaking and crying uncontrollably and felt confused about how much time had actually passed. His wife said he began screaming for help and didn't realize that he was at home and not in Iraq.

Avoidance

Because being reminded of the traumatic event (or events) is so painful, you may find yourself going to great lengths to avoid any reminders. For example, you might not want to talk about or think about the trauma. You might also avoid certain people or places that remind you of the event. For some people, the avoidance runs so deep that they cannot remember important aspects of the event. Also, you might lack interest in life—feeling you are not connecting with people. Many people with PTSD feel numb emotionally, particularly when it comes to positive emotions. Also, you may feel there is no reason to plan for the future, or that you may not live to experience positive things in your life.

CASE EXAMPLE

Carla is a twenty-year-old college student. When she was nineteen years old she was sexually assaulted by the coach of her college basketball team. Prior to the assault, he showed Carla a great deal of attention, often paying her compliments and offering her rides back to her dorm. Carla enjoyed his attention but thought it was harmless flirtation. After the assault, Carla immediately quit the basketball team. She hasn't returned phone calls from her former teammates and she hasn't attended class regularly for over six months. Carla stopped dating and rarely goes out with friends. She used to enjoy watching sports on television, but she avoids it now because it causes her to cry uncontrollably and think about what the coach did to her. Carla feels betrayed, angry, and lonely and says she doubts that she will ever be able trust anyone again, particularly a man.

Feeling Constantly Anxious or on Edge

The final set of symptoms having to do with PTSD has to do with feeling overly anxious, worried, or on edge most of the time. For example, you may have difficulty sleeping and concentrating. Many people with PTSD talk about difficulty managing their anger, or feeling very irritable. You may also be "on guard" a lot of the time, always scanning your environment for a possible threat. Related to this, you might be easily startled or reactive to noises or unexpected changes in your environment.

CASE EXAMPLE

Mike is a forty-five-year-old father of two. Five months ago, while waiting at the train station to go to work, Mike was robbed at gunpoint by a group of four teenagers. Mike was badly beaten during the incident, and he had to be rushed to the emergency room for a concussion after being kicked and punched. Although Mike recovered physically, he had a great deal of trouble returning to work. He tried to take the train again, but found that he was continually examining the faces of the people on the train, worried that someone might harm him. If he felt nervous, he would exit the train or try to enter another car while the train was in motion. On several occasions he ran out of the station and hailed a cab to work. Mike says he's quick to pick fights with people who look at him the wrong way, and that he usually thinks that people are out to hurt him in some way.

Different people experience different symptoms. One way to decide which techniques will work best for you is to figure out which types of symptoms you are experiencing. Worksheet 2 will not give you a diagnosis of PTSD—only a trained professional can provide you with an official diagnosis. Instead, the purpose of this worksheet is to help you decide a) which types of symptoms you are experiencing, and b) which chapters of this workbook will be most helpful for you.

Worksheet 2: What Types of Symptoms Do I Have?

Purpose: To determine what symptoms of trauma you may have, and which exercises it will be most helpful to focus on based on your symptoms.

Instructions: Mark the symptoms below that apply to you. If you have more than one symptom in a cluster, you should focus on the exercises in the relevant chapters for that cluster.

Cluster 1: **Feeling Constantly Anxious or On Edge**	**Relevant Exercises in Chapter 4**
You often have difficulty falling or staying asleep.	____ Yes
You experience intense irritability or anger on a regular basis.	____ Yes
You often have difficulty concentrating.	____ Yes
You feel anxious and worried much of the time, often scanning the environment for threats.	____ Yes
You are easily startled (for example, when you experience unexpected noises or feel threatened).	____ Yes
Cluster 2: **Avoidance**	**Relevant Exercises in Chapter 5**
You try to avoid thoughts, feelings, or conversations that remind you of the traumatic event.	____ Yes
You try to avoid people, places, and situations that remind you of the traumatic event.	____ Yes
You can't recall important aspects of the traumatic event, even if you try.	____ Yes
You are not really interested in things you used to enjoy before the traumatic event.	____ Yes
You don't feel connected or close to other people.	____ Yes
You have trouble experiencing emotions and feelings (for example, you feel emotionally numb).	____ Yes
You rarely make plans for the future (for example, you sometimes think your future will be cut short).	____ Yes

Cluster 3: Re-experiencing	Relevant Exercises in Chapter 6
You have recurrent and upsetting recollections of the event (for example, distressing memories, images, thoughts, and feelings).	____ Yes
You have repeated, upsetting dreams about the event.	____ Yes
There are times when you feel or act as if the event is happening all over again (for example, having flashbacks or images that make you feel you are in the situation all over again; losing your sense of time).	____ Yes
You feel extremely upset when something in the environment, or a thought or feeling in your own mind, reminds you of the event.	____ Yes
Your body reacts when things remind you of the trauma (for example, sweating, heart racing, light-headedness, upset stomach).	____ Yes

How Are Traumatic Memories Processed?

Part of the key to understanding how we react to traumatic events is to look a little closer at how these memories are processed. It is probably obvious that we don't remember every single second of every day. Normal memory isn't like a video recorder. Let's say you park your car in a large parking lot and go to a meeting. An hour later, you'd have a lot of trouble remembering the color of the car parked next to you. It is true that you probably saw the car, but it is unlikely that you encoded or remembered any sort of information about it. After all, the car color probably isn't an emotionally charged memory. It is just an everyday event.

Trauma memories are different. These events are not run of the mill. They are frightening, horrible, and emotionally upsetting. Before a traumatic event you probably had some preexisting beliefs about how the world works, such as:

- The world is basically a safe place.

- Life is predictable.

- Horrible things don't happen to good people.

- Really bad things can happen to other people, not me.

The reason trauma memories are so difficult to deal with is that they are highly emotionally charged and they go against our beliefs about how the world works. You may be replaying a traumatic event over and over again in your mind to find a way to understand how it could have happened—trying to fit it into your belief system (Cahill and Foa 2007). When you cannot find a way to understand what has happened to you, you may experience anxiety, depression, shame, and guilt (Janoff-Bulman 2002).

Another reason that trauma memories are so difficult to deal with is that they may actually be stored in different parts of the brain and coded differently than regular memories (LeDoux 1992). Some parts of a traumatic event are processed consciously and are *verbally accessible*. Verbally accessible information is information you easily remember about where you were, what you were doing, and how you reacted after a traumatic event. There is also a portion of the event that is processed nonconsciously—out of your awareness. These emotionally charged memories are *situationally accessible*, meaning you have less control over when and how you remember them. They are often triggered when something reminds you of the traumatic event. People, places, smells, sounds, and feelings can all remind you of these types of trauma memories. These situationally accessible memories are often rich in detail; they were processed rapidly by the brain during the time of the actual traumatic event (Brewin, Dalgleish, and Joseph 1996). To tackle traumatic memories we need to get a handle on the situationally activated memories (usually these are what people experience as "flashbacks") as well as find a way to integrate our shattered assumptions about the world into a new, coherent belief system. Figure 2 illustrates the relationship between verbally and situationally accessible memories.

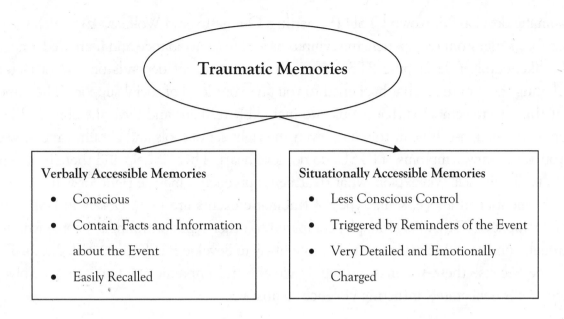

Figure 2: How Trauma Memories Are Stored and Retrieved

People cope with trauma memories in different ways. Some find that the memories play in their minds over and over again. They may find that the verbally accessible memories completely interfere with their life and their ability to function. Others try to avoid the trauma memories at all costs, particularly the situationally accessible memories, which tend to be very detailed and intense. They avoid any situations or thoughts that might bring up these memories. The end result is the same, however: avoidance makes it difficult to lead a happy and healthy life.

Prevalence of PTSD

The good news is that even though traumatic events are common, PTSD is not as common. Eight percent of men and twenty-five percent of women who are exposed to something traumatic develop full-blown PTSD (Kimerling, Ouimette, and Wolfe 2002), which means that they suffer from re-experiencing symptoms and from avoidance and increased anxiety. The likelihood of developing PTSD after a traumatic event depends on lots of factors, including the nature of what happened to you and your level of social support. The important thing to remember is that people are incredibly resilient and have the ability to heal from even the most difficult traumas, given the right set of tools and circumstances. Even if you have many symptoms of PTSD, do not lose heart. There is help and there is healing. This book will help you explore what treatment approaches may be right for you.

As mentioned above, some types of traumatic events are more closely linked to the development of PTSD. For example, compared to other types of traumas, people who live through combat and sexual assault are more likely to develop PTSD (Foa et al. 2000). This may be because these traumas are highly violent and unpredictable, and they involve a perpetrator deliberately inflicting violence against you.

What Are Other Reactions to Traumatic Events?

There are many reactions to traumatic events that are somewhat different from PTSD. These include acute stress and grief reactions, depression, and other types of anxiety reactions. Although the exercises in this book are mainly focused on PTSD, some of the techniques may also be useful for helping you with feelings of depression or anxiety.

Acute Stress and Grief Reactions

A person with *acute stress disorder* has many of the symptoms of PTSD for a period of several weeks after the stressor. It is not a prolonged reaction, and usually it resolves on its own, particularly if you have a good support system and are generally healthy. *Grief reactions* are another way that people may respond to traumatic events. These usually consist of extreme sadness, difficulty maintaining a routine, difficulty concentrating, and problems with guilt and anger. Grief reactions can happen after the sudden, unexpected death of a loved one, and they can last a few weeks or longer. They may also be associated with sudden illness or injury.

Depression

Depression is a common consequence of experiencing a traumatic event. The prevalence of depression varies a lot depending on the type of trauma experienced and the amount of social support available after it happens. Many survivors experience extreme sadness, weight loss or weight gain, difficulty concentrating, and a general loss of interest in things they used to enjoy. This may be accompanied by feelings of guilt, hopelessness, irritability, or anger. Depression can last for several weeks or for much longer periods. Survivor guilt and self-blame are closely related to depression. If you lived through something traumatic and others did not, you may be asking yourself why you survived. Sadly, it is not uncommon for people to feel a sense of guilt and self-blame, thinking about what they could have done differently to prevent the traumatic event or change the outcome.

Other Reactions

Some people who have lived through a traumatic event may have different types of anxiety-related actions. For example, you may have intense periods of fear and anxiety that last approximately five to ten minutes. During these *panic attacks*, you may feel like you are going crazy, fear you are losing control, and experience nausea, dizziness, sweating, and a racing heart. The panic attacks may be cued by something that reminds you of the trauma, or they may come out of the blue. You may also find yourself avoiding situations or going to great lengths to reduce your feelings of anxiety. For example, a combat veteran may avoid standing with his back to the door in a crowded room. He might be afraid that he will not be able to escape in case of an ambush.

Finally, some people may find themselves coping with a traumatic event by using drugs and alcohol. The next chapter will explore issues of substance abuse and coping in greater detail.

Worksheet 3: What Are My Other Symptoms?

Purpose: To help you decide a) if you are experiencing other symptoms related to your trauma, and b) which chapters of this workbook will be most helpful for you.

Instructions: Mark the symptoms below that apply to you. If you are experiencing the symptom listed, focus on the exercises in the relevant chapters.

I have prolonged periods of sadness, crying, and hopelessness.	_____ Yes	Focus on chapters 4 and 5
I am unable to keep up with my routine (for example, go to school, meet deadlines at work, finish tasks around the house).	_____ Yes	Focus on chapters 4 and 5
Sometimes I blame myself for the traumatic event.	_____ Yes	Focus on chapter 4
Sometimes I feel guilty about what I did or didn't do during the traumatic event.	_____ Yes	Focus on chapter 4
I experience periods of intense anxiety that usually peak and subside in a few minutes (panic attacks) and that are associated with the traumatic event.	_____ Yes	Focus on chapters 5 and 6

Conclusion

Many people with PTSD find it difficult to talk about their symptoms and diagnosis. You may feel that thinking about your PTSD makes you feel ashamed, helpless, or alone. But it is important for you to remember that a diagnosis is just a tool. Looking at your symptoms, naming them, and understanding them will help you to choose exercises that can help you to heal. The symptoms don't need to define you and they don't need to control your life.

There is great evidence that people are resilient. There are several factors that predict recovery from a traumatic event:

- Experiencing one rather than several traumatic events in your life

- Having friends and family to support you

- Getting support from people who've been though a similar trauma

- Finding a sense of meaning and purpose for your life

- Feeling that you can handle the challenges of life (a sense of mastery)

- Keeping up your routines and staying involved in daily life

- Using therapy if you have overwhelming symptoms

- Using coping strategies that help you face rather than avoid your fears and symptoms.

Some of these factors are things you cannot change. For example, you cannot control whether you have experienced more than one traumatic event. But there are many other factors that you can influence—for example, your level of social support and your attempts to face your fears. The exercises in chapters 4, 5, and 6 will focus on helping you develop your own resilience.

Chapter 2

Physical and Health Issues Associated with Trauma

The mind and the body are connected. When you've experienced something traumatic, it's natural for it to take a toll on your mental health as well as your physical health. Traumatic events may lead us to cope with our stress in unhealthy ways, which may in turn lead to long-term, negative health effects. For example, trauma survivors might turn to smoking, overeating, drinking alcohol, or using drugs to cope with their negative emotions. These behaviors provide a certain amount of short-term relief from the pain of negative emotions. However, in the long term, they lead to dangerous diseases like obesity, heart disease, and cancer. Overall, the way you cope with trauma can definitely have an effect on your physical health.

Why Trauma Affects Physical Health

There are two main pathways through which trauma can influence your physical health. The first way is through negative coping behaviors, which take a toll on your body over the long term. Over the course of years and decades, smoking, overeating, using drugs and alcohol, or having risky sex have terrible effects. Compared to people who haven't experienced trauma, survivors report higher levels of chronic pain, gastrointestinal disorders, lung and breathing problems, gynecological problems, and fibromyalgia (Letourneau et al. 1999; Sadler et al. 2000). Survivors also have higher rates of obesity (Perkonigg et al. 2009). People who have experienced multiple traumatic events have more physical health problems than those who have experienced one traumatic event (Dennis et al. 2009). The relationship between mental health and physical health is strong. Compared to people who don't visit their medical doctor very often, people who visit their physician often are twice as likely to have a diagnosis of PTSD (Deykin et al. 2001).

The Adverse Childhood Experience (ACE) Survey was a very large study that looked at how childhood experiences affected people's physical and mental health (Felitti et al. 1998). The researchers looked at over 13,000 patients in a large health maintenance organization (HMO) in the United States. An "adverse childhood event" was defined as an experience of any of the following before the age of eighteen:

- Recurrent physical abuse

- Recurrent emotional abuse

- Sexual abuse

- An alcohol and/or drug abuser in your household

- An incarcerated household member

- A household member who is chronically depressed, mentally ill, institutionalized, or suicidal

- Your mother being treated violently in your household

Participants were given one point for each of these adverse childhood experiences, with the total yielding their ACE score. The researchers found that compared to people with an ACE score of 0, participants with a score of 4 or more were 60 percent more likely to suffer from depression, 260 percent more likely to suffer from lung problems (likely due to their high rates of smoking), and 250 percent more likely to have a sexually transmitted disease. This was a very powerful study suggesting that people don't just "get over" traumatic events, particularly multiple traumas. Learning to deal with your trauma symptoms can help both your physical and mental health. So we can say that:

Traumatic events → mental health consequences → unhealthy coping → long-term physical health consequences

The second way that trauma influences health is through actual physiological changes in your brain. Over time, there may be biological changes due to chronic stress. Certain symptoms of PTSD actually cause changes in your body. For example, the increased arousal and re-experiencing symptoms (see worksheet 2) have been associated with increased blood pressure, and eventually with heart problems and poor physical health (Kimerling, Clum, and Wolfe 2000; Zoellner, Goodwin, and Foa 2000). People who have lived through traumatic events show neurological differences when they deal with stress. The amygdala, a part of the brain that is involved with emotional arousal, seems to show more activity in trauma survivors. Trauma survivors also seem to have higher base levels of cortisol, a hormone related to stress (Dutton et al. 2006; Ganzel et al. 2007). Over the long term, these biological changes may make you more vulnerable to heart disease and other chronic health problems. So we can say that:

Traumatic events → changes in brain and body chemistry → physical reactions → long-term physical health consequences

So how do we put all of this together? The figure below represents the complex relationship between traumatic events, coping, and mental and physical health. As you can see, traumatic events are related to brain and body reactions, ways of coping, and, eventually, physical health problems. Unhealthy coping is related to a risk of additional trauma, which of course makes it more likely you will experience biological and brain changes. The basic point of figure 3 is that if you can work on how you cope with stress and deal more effectively with your PTSD symptoms, you are more likely to avoid the long-term negative health effects of trauma.

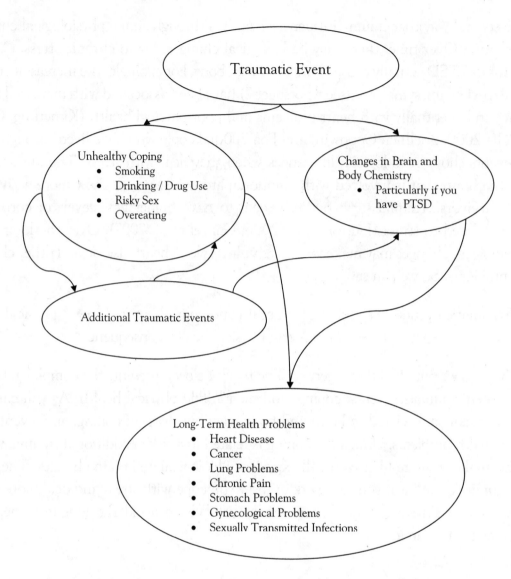

Figure 3: Traumatic Events, Coping, Biology, and Physical Health

Thinking about Coping

Everyone has ways that they cope with stress. It's easy to fall into a trap of thinking that some types of coping are good (for example, exercise) and some are bad (for example, smoking). In truth, thinking about things in this way doesn't get you very far. You usually feel guilty for choosing "bad" ways to cope, which makes you feel worse about yourself, and then you are even more likely to feel stressed (thus setting up a cycle of "bad" coping). Instead, try to think of coping as "helpful" or "harmful." That is, some types of coping work to keep you healthy and other types of coping are harmful to your health and your long-term goals.

Unfortunately, there is evidence that experiencing traumatic events increases your chances of using maladaptive coping methods. In fact, trauma survivors are more likely than non–trauma survivors to drink alcohol, use drugs, smoke cigarettes, overeat, and practice unsafe sex (Breiding, Black, and Ryan 2008; Felitti et al. 1998). Depending on the specific type of maladaptive coping, it is possible that you may become even more vulnerable to future trauma. For example, if you are drinking to try to escape your emotions about a sexual assault you survived as a teenager, you may be more likely to become exposed to an unsafe situation and be assaulted again as an adult. This doesn't mean it is your fault and it doesn't mean you asked for it. What it means is that this way of coping (in this case, substance use) is not working to keep you healthy and safe. Similarly, there is evidence that trauma survivors are less likely to practice safer sex than nontraumatized individuals. This might seem strange at first, but it makes sense when we look at the deeper issues involved. For example, a woman who has experienced sexual assault and domestic violence may not feel confident in her ability to negotiate condom use and sexual boundaries with a partner. Instead, she might avoid thinking about sex and sexuality entirely—clearly making a discussion of safer sex practices with her partners quite difficult. Unsafe sex behaviors might expose her to future traumatic events, including the diagnosis of HIV. So we can say that:

Traumatic events → unhealthy coping → increased chances of future trauma

Preventative Health Services

When it comes to survivors taking care of their health, the data seem to show something very inconsistent going on. On one hand, compared to others, trauma survivors use a lot of medical services. They tend to go to the doctor and emergency room more often, and experience a greater number of physical health problems. This is true no matter how you get the health information—if you ask patients directly, if you look at their labs or medical chart, or if you ask their doctors (Ouimette et al. 2004; Wagner et al. 2000). A diagnosis of PTSD (compared to simply being a survivor of a traumatic event) makes it even more likely that you experience a lot of health problems. But on the other hand, people who have survived traumatic events are also much less likely to take advantage of preventative medical care. So for example, you might be avoiding getting regular mammograms, cervical cancer screenings, or dental appointments.

So what is going on here? Maybe it is difficult for you to face a medical appointment where you know you might feel out of control and your body will be touched. Some of the exercises in the book will help you manage those feelings of anxiety and helplessness. There is also a chance that your medical providers do not know that you have experienced a traumatic event. It's important for you to find ways to communicate about your needs, even if you decide not to go into the details of your experiences (we'll talk about this in chapter 8). It is very important for you to consider this issue in order to get the support you need and the long-term health you deserve. In summary, you cannot separate your mental health from your physical health. You need to look at both issues so you can develop resilience and live the life you truly want. Worksheets 4 and 5 will help you take a look at how you are coping and how to know if you need more help.

Worksheet 4: How Am I Coping?

Purpose: To think about how you are coping with stress, and to determine whether your coping mechanisms are healthy or unhealthy ones.

Instructions: Think back to how you have dealt with stress this past week. Write down a few sentences about how you have been feeling and what you have done to cope with those feelings. Then take a look at what you have written, and try to decide what is adaptive and what is maladaptive coping—that is, what is healthy and what is unhealthy.

Example:

What happened, how I felt, and how I coped: *On Monday I felt really tired after my boss yelled at me at work. The way he was disrespecting me reminded me of how my ex-husband used to treat me. It brought back all the memories of hitting and screaming. I felt so awful—I smoked a few cigarettes on the way home. I ordered a pizza for dinner, watched TV, and didn't pick up the phone when my daughter called. On Thursday I was feeling a lot more upbeat. I actually went out to lunch with my friend—which was really nice. It was good to laugh.*

My healthy coping: *getting support from my friend, humor and laughing*

My unhealthy coping: *eating greasy food when I wasn't that hungry; smoking; isolating myself*

Exercise:

What happened, how I felt, and how I coped:

My healthy coping:

My unhealthy coping:

Seeking Help

Worksheet 5 will help you to decide if you need more help. In general, if you are using drugs and alcohol to cope, if you are engaging in risky sex, or if you are dealing with strong feelings of anger or thoughts of suicide, you should seek more assistance as soon as possible. Dealing with trauma and PTSD can be very difficult, and in conjunction with some of these other issues, it can be very challenging to deal with alone. There is no shame or stigma in seeking help. Remember, resilient individuals are those who know when to turn to others. Chapter 7 will give you more information about how to choose a professional who is right for you. You can still use this book as a guide to healing, but a trained professional may help you through it, particularly if you are dealing with many of the symptoms in worksheet 5.

Worksheet 5: Do I Need More Help?

Purpose: To find out if you may need the help of a trained professional to deal with your symptoms.

Instructions: Check the answers that apply to you. If you check off any answers that are next to an asterisk (*), you should consider consulting a professional about your treatment plan.

How often do you drink alcohol to cope with stress?	Rarely (less than a few times a year) ____ Sometimes (once a month or so) ____ * Often (every week or almost every week) ____ *
Has alcohol use caused you difficulty in keeping up with your work or school, or in your relationships?	No ____ Yes ____ *
Have friends, family, or your doctor expressed concerns about your alcohol use?	No ____ Yes ____ *
Have you had trouble with the law because of alcohol use?	No ____ Yes ____ *
How often do you use drugs (prescription or nonprescription) to cope with stress?	Rarely (less than a few times a year) ____ Sometimes (once a month or so) ____ * Often (every week or almost every week) ____ *
Has drug use caused you difficulty in keeping up with your work or school, or in your relationships?	No ____ Yes ____ *
Have friends, family, or your doctor expressed concerns about your drug use?	No ____ Yes ____ *
Have you had trouble with the law because of drug use?	No ____ Yes ____ *

Have you ever engaged in risky or unprotected sex?	No ____
	Yes ____ *
Have you ever threatened someone with physical violence?	No ____
	Yes ____ *
Have you ever hurt someone physically?	No ____
	Yes ____ *
Have you had serious thoughts of hurting yourself?	No ____
	Yes ____ *
Have you ever attempted suicide?	No ____
	Yes ____ *

Conclusion

PTSD and trauma can definitely take a toll on your physical health. It is important to pay close attention to the ways you are dealing with your feelings of depression, anxiety, guilt, or self-blame. In the long term, using drugs and alcohol, smoking, overeating, or engaging in risky sex can harm your health in many ways. The exercises in this workbook, along with professional assistance, can help you to find alternative ways to cope with negative feelings so you can live a longer, healthier life.

Part 2

Integrating Current Therapeutic Techniques into Your Life

Chapter 3

Understanding Current Evidence-Based Therapies

If you are struggling with the aftereffects of trauma, including symptoms of PTSD, you may be quite relieved to know that in the last several decades, there have been huge advances in finding techniques to help you. Historically, the road hasn't been easy for survivors of trauma. After World War II, psychologists, psychiatrists, and the general public did not understand why soldiers who had experienced combat had such a difficult time adjusting back to life after the war. Soldiers often reported feeling distant from other people and sometimes suffered from flashbacks and nightmares about their combat experiences. This syndrome was first known to the public as "shell shock" (Jones and Wessely 2006). In general, there was little understanding or knowledge about our reactions to life-threatening situations. After the Vietnam War, there was a renewed interest in helping people who had survived traumatic events. Since that time, mental health professionals have begun to understand the common ways people cope with various traumatic events, from combat to assault to natural disasters. There has been a strong effort to help people recover and live a life that is not limited by PTSD symptoms (Andreasen 2010).

What Is an Evidence-Based Treatment?

Some treatments for PTSD have been developed and tested in a structured and systematic way. We call these treatments "evidence-based." Basically, to meet this standard, it is not enough for people to say that they like their therapist's personality or that they generally feel better when they are in therapy. Of course, these are very important things! However, evidence-based treatment goes further. People who complete evidence-based treatments experience more improvement in their symptoms and function better, on average, than people who have not had treatment. Basically, the treatments have been studied using well-established methods and they have been shown to be effective with many kinds of people and trauma types. The goal of these therapies goes beyond providing simple support—the focus is on reducing your symptoms and, ultimately, enabling you to live a healthier and more productive life.

In this chapter we will talk about the three types of therapy discussed in this book—therapies that can help with PTSD symptoms: cognitive behavioral therapy (CBT), dialectical behavior therapy (DBT), and acceptance and commitment therapy (ACT). CBT is an evidence-based therapy for PTSD. The other two, DBT and ACT, have not been examined specifically for PTSD, but they use various techniques that look very promising for PTSD symptoms. For example, ACT has been used successfully to treat anxiety, and DBT has been used to help people deal with difficulties managing their mood and forming close relationships.

Each of these therapies contains key assumptions about how people change; each also has some central techniques. We will review specific CBT, DBT, and ACT skills and discuss what these approaches have in common. By understanding the basics, you can begin to see which approaches fit best for you and decide which evidence-based techniques you want to try. Becoming educated is an important first step in regaining some control over your symptoms and your life.

Cognitive Behavioral Therapy

Cognitive behavioral therapy focuses on people's thoughts, feelings, and emotions (Barlow 2007). It is based on a few key assumptions:

- Thoughts, feelings, emotions, and physical reactions are all related. If we change one, we can make changes in the others.

- Change happens in small steps, not all at once.

- Behavior change is a skill—it requires practice and is not just a question of deciding to do something.

- Judging our behavior as "good or bad" doesn't get us anywhere. It is more useful to think about how our behavior fits in with our overall goals, as "helpful or not helpful" or "healthy or unhealthy."

AN EXAMPLE OF CBT

Let's take a look at what CBT looks like when it's actually applied. This example has to do with feeling sad and depressed, emotions that often accompany PTSD. Maybe a well-meaning friend says to you, "You need to snap out of this depression—it's not good for you to be this down all the time." The truth is, if you could wave a magic wand and feel better, you would! Emotions are not easy to change, but often, changing our thoughts and our behaviors can help us to change our emotions. We can describe the links between thoughts, behaviors, emotions, and physical reactions this way:

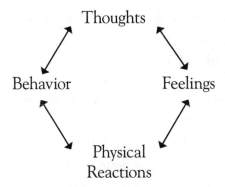

If you are depressed, your emotions may be getting in the way of your daily functioning. Maybe you want to get up in the morning, make yourself a healthy breakfast, and run errands. Perhaps you have a long-term goal of finding a new job because you dislike your current boss. This can all feel pretty overwhelming when you are depressed. Where do you start? A CBT approach helps you break down your longer-term goals into smaller ones. Maybe the manageable behavioral change is to try to get out of bed, brush your teeth, and change your clothes by 8 a.m., three times this week. You begin to notice that after making this small behavior change for two weeks, you feel less depressed and a little more alert by 9 a.m. You think to yourself, "I might actually be able to find a new job in the next few months." This example illustrates how modest behavior changes can start to break the vicious cycle among negative thoughts, unhealthy behaviors, and feelings.

SPECIFIC CBT APPROACHES TO PTSD

There are several CBT techniques that are used to effectively treat PTSD. These include behavioral coping, exposure, stress inoculation, and cognitive processing techniques.

Behavioral Coping. Behavioral coping skills provide the foundation for all CBT approaches to PTSD. You are probably worried that if you let yourself experience negative feelings and emotions, you will become completely overwhelmed by them. People often fear that if they allow themselves to be reminded of the trauma, they will become so anxious, depressed, or angry that they will be unable to function. Because this is a very legitimate concern, all CBT approaches emphasize ways to cope with difficult thoughts and feelings. These coping skills include grounding techniques and relaxation and breathing exercises (see worksheets 7 through 10). All of these skills share a common thread. When you are emotionally overwhelmed, grounding skills help you regain your focus on the present moment and remind yourself that you are currently safe. Relaxation and breathing techniques can serve the same purpose. These techniques are particularly useful when you are reminded of the traumatic event and during painful flashbacks.

Exposure Therapy. One approach that is often used in CBT to address fear, anxiety, and avoidance is exposure therapy. Don't let the name scare you! The fact is that people with PTSD often spend lots of time and energy avoiding people, places, and things that remind them of the traumatic experience (or experiences) that they have survived. You can avoid increasing your anxiety and retriggering your symptoms by trying to avoid any reminders of the trauma. In the short term, avoidance strategies work fairly well. In the long term, however, these strategies can cause your life to become very limited.

The basic premise of exposure therapy is that if you can talk about your traumatic experience in small, planned, and manageable portions, you will eventually be able to cope with your emotions and deal effectively with trauma-related triggers (Friedman 2003). You will no longer need to avoid people, places, and thoughts because you will feel confident that you can manage your associated feelings. Exposure techniques are based on the basic psychological principle of *systematic desensitization*. Trauma-related thoughts and memories cause strong physical reactions and negative emotions. However, those thoughts will eventually lose their power if they are paired with new physical reactions. Eventually, the change in your physical reactions will lead to more manageable emotions. Basically, a new link between your thoughts, feelings, and physical reactions will eventually be formed (Foa, Hembree, and Olaslov 2007).

There are few important things to know before you begin exposure-based techniques. First of all, you don't just jump into exposure therapy. Before taking on those difficult feelings, you need to learn some good coping skills. The exercises in chapter 4 focus on laying the groundwork for exposure-based treatments. You would never jump in the deep end of a pool without learning how to tread water. Similarly, you never start exposure techniques without good preparation. Second, you are in control of the process. Exposure therapy isn't something someone else can "do" to you. You will select what you want to focus on, what you feel you can manage, and when you are ready to work. Swimming in deeper emotional water feels scary and overwhelming at first, but you will know when you are prepared. The exercises in this book have prompts that will help you to determine if exposure-based techniques will benefit you. Finally, exposure-based techniques can take many forms, including talking about the trauma, writing about the trauma, or actually confronting (in small steps) situations that remind you of the traumatic event. Exposure-based treatments are particularly helpful in managing environmental trauma triggers, like sights, sounds, and smells connected with the event. They are also useful in dealing with nightmares and flashbacks. Overall, exposure therapy has been looked at in many studies of people with PTSD and seems to be very effective (Powers et al. 2010).

So how does exposure treatment actually work? Here's an example. Betty was sexually assaulted as a freshman in college. She had gone on a date with Mike, a man who lived in her dorm. Initially, he was very persistent in pursuing her and flirting with her. Betty felt very flattered by his attention. On the date, they went to a party, and both of them had several drinks. When they were alone together, Mike began to pressure Betty to have sex with him. When Betty refused, he became extremely angry and rough, and sexually assaulted her. Understandably, Betty becomes extremely upset when she sees anyone who looks like Mike. She has not dated since the assault, feels highly anxious, and has flashbacks of the rape, particularly when she is alone in her dorm room.

Betty and her therapist decide to use exposure-based approaches in her treatment. First, Betty learns some coping skills to deal with difficult feelings. She decides to use some breathing techniques and learns grounding skills (see worksheets 7, 10, 13, and 18). When she is ready, she decides to tell her therapist the details of her assault. The first few times Betty talks about the details of what she lived through, it is extremely difficult. She needs to spend an hour afterward breathing and working through her difficult feelings and emotions. Betty and her therapist have carefully planned what she is going to do for the rest of the day, and she has made sure a friend is available to talk to her if she needs support. Betty finds that after talking about the incident again and again and again in sessions with her therapist, she is slowly able to cope with how she feels. She is no longer completely overwhelmed by her emotional reactions. The memory of the assault is always going to be very sad and unpleasant for Betty. But after using exposure-based techniques, the incident no longer has the same power over her. After several months, Betty no longer breaks down in tears when she has memories of the assault. Her heart no longer races uncontrollably when she thinks about that night. She is able to go out with her friends and is no longer terrified of being alone in her room. Exposure-based treatments don't make the difficult memories disappear, but the technique does help to make the pain of the memories more manageable. Consequently, it means that you do not have to spend great amounts of time and energy avoiding your trauma-related reminders.

One final note about exposure-based treatments. You may have heard of a technique called EMDR (which stands for *eye movement desensitization and reprocessing*). This technique calls for you to move your eyes back and forth rapidly while talking about a traumatic event. Variants of the treatment use alternating sounds. Interestingly, this type of treatment does seem to be effective. However, at this time, there is little evidence that the eye movements add to treatment. Basically, this treatment may work because it is based on exposure and processing of traumatic memories (Foa et al. 2000). This book will present exposure-based exercises, but will not include all the aspects of EMDR treatment.

Stress Inoculation Training (SIT). Based on the work of Donald Michenbaum (2007), *stress inoculation training* (SIT) focuses specifically on the anxiety and fear that people with PTSD struggle with on a daily basis. It helps you to develop an awareness of what triggers your anxiety and flashbacks. The first phase of treatment focuses on learning relaxation skills, breathing, and looking at the ways that you think about the trauma. You can use imagery to visualize yourself successfully dealing with trauma-related triggers. You can also practice what you might say when confronted with a difficult situation, for example how to respond when you feel threatened or vulnerable. Overall, the goal of this approach is to use your coping skills to plan for and prevent overwhelming emotional reactions to trauma-related triggers.

Here is an example of SIT in action. John is a thirty-year-old who recently got a new job. On his way to work, he was grazed by a bullet during a drive-by shooting. He was an innocent bystander caught in gang crossfire. After the shooting, John finds it impossible to go to work. He was not seriously injured physically, but he is overcome with anxiety. Every time John drives his car his palms start sweating and his heart races. His thoughts start to feel out of control and he thinks, "This is it, I am going to die. I am going to be shot again." Unfortunately, John's high level of anxiety doesn't seem to subside in the weeks and months after the trauma. He decides to use SIT techniques to manage his emotions. First, he learns some deep breathing and progressive muscle relaxation techniques. Using a rating scale of 1 to 100, he learns to identify the situations where his anxiety becomes the highest. For example, when he is at a stop light and a car pulls up next to him (particularly if the driver is male), he feels a very high level of anxiety and panic. After John has identified this trigger, he uses breathing techniques to calm himself down when driving. He also begins to notice when his shoulders are tight and his jaws and fists begin to clench with anxiety. By learning to relax them, he is better able to cope with his anxiety. His thoughts slowly begin to change from "I am going to die" to "If something unexpected happens to me, I will know how to survive it. I can handle it." After several months of using these techniques, John begins to feel a certain sense of control when he drives. Although he is still nervous when traveling to a new area, he is able to travel locally with only a mild level of anxiety.

Cognitive Processing Therapy (CPT). *Cognitive processing therapy* was developed by Resick and Schnicke (1992) specifically to treat PTSD after sexual assault. However, over the years it has been applied to various types of trauma. Recently it has been widely adopted by the Veterans Administration for use in VA hospitals to treat military as well as sexual trauma (Monson et al. 2006). The basic structure of CPT involves writing about the traumatic event and reading the account repeatedly in sessions with your therapist. In many ways, this is like exposure-based treatments. The written account should include information about how the trauma influenced your view about yourself, others, and the world in general. Together, you and your therapist identify stuck points, which are thoughts that involve powerlessness, self-blame, and guilt. When you can identify and slowly change unhelpful thoughts about safety, trust, power, self-esteem, and intimacy, you may experience less depression and a greater sense of connection with others.

Here is an example of CPT. Amanda is a nurse who was recently honorably discharged from the Marines. She served three tours of duty in Iraq and Afghanistan. Amanda saw a great deal of death and suffering when she was stationed at various military hospitals overseas. However, she struggles with one incident that was particularly distressing. She remembers a mother and her four children being brought in for treatment. All the children had been badly burned after they had been caught in the crossfire of a mortar attack at the local market. She vividly remembers the children's faces, which were full of pain and anguish. Amanda is overcome with guilt and sadness, remembering how she had to tell the two surviving siblings that their sisters were dead. Amanda decides to use a CPT approach to help her deal with this very painful memory. After writing about it several times, she realizes that her major stuck points involve thoughts like "I didn't do enough to help those children" and "Kids should never be casualties of war." Amanda learns to challenge the first thought by thinking about all she did do to save the sisters. She gradually rewrites her story to include all the efforts she made to revive the children, and to comfort them when they were suffering. The second stuck point is more difficult to challenge. Certainly a belief that children should not suffer the wounds of war seems reasonable. However, the injustice of it all has kept Amanda overwhelmed in sorrow. She gradually learns to replace this belief with "Kids should never be the casualties of war, but unfortunately, sometimes they are. But as a nurse I've done my absolute best to help as many children as possible and I will continue to do so." As you can see, CPT can be particularly useful when people are dealing with guilt and self-blame.

Dialectical Behavior Therapy

Dialectical behavior therapy (DBT), developed by Marsha Linehan (1993), is a treatment that has great promise for the treatment for trauma. It has been used very effectively to help people who have difficulty managing emotions and forming close relationships, and with people who have thoughts of hurting themselves. Dialectical behavior therapy emphasizes emotions—particularly how we learn to deal with difficult feelings. If you've ever found yourself overwhelmed with difficult emotions, and if those emotions interfere with your relationships, DBT may be very useful to you. It is based on the following assumptions:

- If your emotional reactions are disregarded (by your caregivers) when you are young, you may have difficulty identifying, labeling, and dealing with your emotions as an adult.

- When you have difficulty managing your emotions, it takes a toll on your relationships with others.

- We often increase our level of distress by thinking about what has already happened and what may happen in the future.

- Mindfulness skills, which are a set of techniques that help you to come back to the present moment, can help you manage distressing emotions and thoughts.

- Sometimes it works to try to change negative emotions, and other times it works to accept those difficult emotions. You can develop skills to help decide which approach to take in various situations.

Dialectical behavior therapy treatment was originally developed to treat borderline personality disorder. People who are diagnosed with borderline personality disorder often have difficulty with relationships and frequently have a history of suicidal thoughts and actions. In recent years, DBT has been used to approach a variety of conditions, including PTSD (Becker and Zayfert 2001). This mode of therapy consists of several aspects: mindfulness skills, interpersonal effectiveness, emotion regulation, and distress tolerance.

MINDFULNESS SKILLS

Mindfulness is a concept that is based on Eastern religious traditions, including Buddhism (Kabat-Zinn 1994; Follette, Palm, and Pearson 2006). Mindfulness helps you build an awareness of the present moment, focusing your attention on your emotions, thoughts, and bodily sensations. It requires paying attention to what is going on, observing and describing your experiences, but doing so without judgment. Bringing the concept of mindfulness into psychology was quite revolutionary. Cognitive behavioral therapy, for example, generally has a focus on changing thoughts and emotions, whereas mindfulness simply focuses on developing awareness. Interestingly, developing mindfulness skills can help you deal with flashbacks and negative emotions. By paying attention to what is going on in the present moment, you can learn to ground yourself and better deal with PTSD symptoms (Becker and Zayfert 2001). Worksheets 10, 12, 13, 18, and 25 are focused on developing mindfulness.

Here is an example of how mindfulness can help you deal with PTSD symptoms. Janet is a survivor of childhood sexual abuse. She was molested by a neighbor on three separate occasions when she was eight years old. When Janet told her mother about the abuse, her mother refused to believe it, saying Janet "must have misunderstood what happened." She told Janet that their neighbor was a respected member of the local community and that he loved children. The neighbor moved away when Janet was nine, but Janet believes the abuse and her mother's reaction took a toll on her feelings of self-worth. When Janet was nineteen, she married a man who became very physically abusive toward her and her children. At the age of twenty-six, Janet divorced her husband. She now supports her children, ages five and eight, without any financial help from her ex-husband. Janet was recently promoted to an executive assistant position at the law firm she has worked in for years. The position is exciting and has a lot of responsibilities. However, Janet is dealing with times when she has extreme difficulty concentrating. She says her mind feels "foggy and dazed," and she's worried that her inability to focus is going to get her fired. Janet has decided to use some mindfulness techniques to help her regain her concentration and focus at work. She practices a number of techniques and finds that exercises that appeal to her sense of touch help her the most. When she feels herself thinking about the abuse and becoming dazed, Janet puts both her feet squarely on the floor. She concentrates on feeling the hard surface of her desk and keyboard. She runs her fingers over a marble paperweight she keeps on her desk, which feels cold and smooth. After a minute or so of concentrating on these sensations, Janet is able to remind herself that she is no longer a nine-year-old girl, and that she no longer lives with her abusive ex-husband. She is able to ground herself in the present moment, which is one of safety, and eventually move toward calmness.

INTERPERSONAL EFFECTIVENESS

Your relationships with other people can be a source of a lot of challenges when you have PTSD. You may feel you are constantly fighting with people, have difficulty connecting with people you love, or continually feel disappointed by others. It is important to remember that in each interaction we have with others, we are juggling various priorities (Linehan 1993). Sometimes our relationship with the other person is the most important thing, sometimes we want to achieve a certain outcome, and sometimes our self-respect is what we value the most. Dialectical behavior therapy skills can help you figure out what your priorities are; note that priorities can change from interaction to interaction. Once you decide on what your goal is, you can use various techniques to get there. For example, if reaching your objective is the most important thing (let's say you want a raise), you should use assertive communication skills and present a fair and balanced argument. If your main goal is to preserve a relationship (for example, if you are having an upsetting fight with your sister), you would communicate using a lot of empathy and understanding. Finally, if you are in a situation where your self-respect is compromised (for example, if someone asks you to lie), you remember your own values and attempt to stick to them without apologies. Worksheets 21, 27, and 31 contain suggestions for improving your interpersonal effectiveness.

Interpersonal effectiveness takes practice. For example, Janet finds that her new boss is often frustrated with her work. He wants a higher level of detail in her reports and Janet feels he is micromanaging her. Janet realizes that her priority in this case is creating a good relationship with her boss. More documentation doesn't compromise her self-respect, and getting her way is less important than getting along with her boss. Thus, Janet decides to use listening skills to make her boss feel she is hearing his point of view. After the two of them meet, they are able to come up with a compromise wherein Janet provides details on certain types of reports, but is able to use her own shorthand for other, less official documentation.

EMOTION REGULATION

Emotions can feel overwhelming. You may find yourself in situations where you have an uncontrollable amount of anxiety, anger, or sadness. There are times when you may feel particularly vulnerable to emotions, for example when you are hungry, tired, or sick. You may also become emotional if you drink too much alcohol or use drugs. One way to better manage your emotions is to make sure you address these issues regularly. You can think of sleep, exercise, good nutrition, and cutting back on mood-altering substances as a basic foundation for mood management (Linehan 1993). Once that foundation is sound, you can decide how to handle difficult emotions. You can do this by learning to judge whether your emotions are justified or are out of proportion to the situation. This will help you decide whether you want to try some active coping and problem solving, or practice some acceptance of the emotions (see the distress tolerance section below). For example, we talked about Janet in the sections above. As part of using emotion regulation skills, Janet learns that she needs to eat breakfast on weekdays. She also finds that taking a brisk walk for five or ten minutes during her break helps her feel less emotionally vulnerable during the day, particularly when she is talking with her boss.

DISTRESS TOLERANCE

Distress tolerance skills help you manage moments of very intense emotions (Linehan 1993). You might decide you want to distract yourself from emotional pain by doing things you enjoy or taking time out from a difficult situation. You can also diffuse your emotions by comparing yourself to others who have less, rather than those who have more. Of course, there are times when no amount of distraction is going to be useful, helpful, or even possible. During these times, it is useful to think about ways to soothe yourself. Different techniques work for different people. These include using imagery, prayer, relaxation, and breathing. You can also use positive self-talk to get you through the difficult times. Finally, when distraction and soothing don't work, there is acceptance. Acceptance can be a very difficult concept to accept! Basically, the theory behind DBT holds that we when we struggle to change difficult emotions and can't seem to do so, we add to our level of suffering.

To build on our previous example, Janet struggles with periods of loneliness. Because she is a single mother and works full time, she has very little time and energy to date men. Sometimes, after her children go to bed, she feels overwhelmingly sad and disappointed. During these moods, Janet often says to herself, "What is wrong with you? Plenty of people raise kids alone—and you don't see them moping around all the time." This leads Janet to feel guilty and ashamed of herself. However, using DBT techniques, Janet learns to identify her primary emotion (sadness) and not add to her suffering by causing a secondary emotion (shame). By accepting her sadness, Janet finds that her periods of feeling down don't last as long. She is surprised to find that by allowing herself to feel sad, she actually is able to recover more quickly. On some evenings, she even has energy to send e-mail to close friends—something she was never able to do when she felt ashamed and guilty.

Acceptance and Commitment Therapy

Acceptance and commitment therapy (ACT) is a form of treatment that helps people observe their thoughts and emotions without judgment (Hayes, Strosahl, and Wilson 1999). It emphasizes the need to identify your values and take action, regardless of your internal state (your thoughts or feelings). Acceptance and commitment therapy does not focus on trying to change thoughts or feelings, but it does emphasize how changing your behavior can help you live a happier life. This type of therapy helps you develop *psychological flexibility*, which is the ability to see things from various viewpoints and react to stressful situations with resilience. Acceptance and commitment therapy is based on the following assumptions:

- We can learn to observe our thoughts, emotions, and traumatic memories without becoming overly involved in their content.

- Accepting our thoughts and feelings reduces our emotional suffering because we are not trying (in vain) to change our internal states.

- Mindfulness is a skill that can help you as you practice acceptance.

- There is a part of you (your true self) that is separate from your thoughts or actions. Some people might call this their "soul" or their essence.

- It is important to identify what you truly value and then work to act in ways that are in line with those values.

ACCEPTANCE

Acceptance is perhaps the most difficult ACT skill, for many reasons. First of all, when you suffer from PTSD, you may feel that "accepting" how you feel will doom you to a life of emotional pain. You may also feel that acceptance—from a psychological standpoint—means giving up on trying to improve your life. This is simply not true. Acceptance is a willingness to experience your emotions. Often, avoidance of emotion and thoughts is at the core of PTSD. By allowing yourself to experience things, you are opening the door to healing.

How might this process work? Let's take the example of Brian. Brian is an army veteran who was recently discharged from the military. He served three tours of duty in Iraq and Afghanistan. Brian was seriously injured during the war. One hot day in August, his unit was attacked by a suicide bomber while they were patrolling the streets of a local neighborhood. His face was badly scarred and his left leg needed to be amputated below the knee. Brian spent three months in a military rehabilitation hospital, and then went home to the care of his wife. When he returned home Brian began drinking regularly as a way to escape his memories of the war. Brian has been unable to find work and refuses to attend a support group for injured veterans. He feels that being around veterans "depresses him and bring up bad memories." He also has a very difficult time going outdoors in the summer. He says that the hot sun and humidity trigger painful flashbacks to Iraq. Brian and his therapist decide to see if ACT techniques will be helpful to him. The first thing Brian must do is to decide he is willing to allow himself to experience his emotions. Brian agrees to cut back his drinking from four beers to two beers a night. As he does this, he experiences a rush of negative emotions, including anger, disappointment, and fear. Although this is a difficult state for Brian to accept, he and his therapist agree that avoiding his emotions has not worked effectively. Brian is hoping that experiencing his emotions without pushing them away is the first step toward healing.

MINDFULNESS

The mindfulness skills in ACT are very similar to those found in DBT. Learning to notice the present moment and pay attention to your internal state is a key component of mindfulness. Your thoughts and feelings are key components of your internal state. When you learn to pay attention without pushing them away (acceptance) you will decrease your avoidance behaviors. Remember, avoiding people, places, and things that remind you of the traumatic event (or events) may be taking a large toll on your quality of life.

In Brian's case, once he began to practice mindfulness to notice his internal states, he became able to observe slight differences in his internal state, and this actually helps to calm him down. For example, he notices that the summer sun in his hometown is often accompanied by the feeling of a cool breeze on his skin. When he takes a few moments to really pay attention to this sensation, he is able to remind himself that he is no longer in Iraq, but is instead safe in his backyard with his wife. Paying attention to the moment actually helps him differentiate between the sensations he felt during the war and the sensations he feels at home. Once he is able to make some of these subtle distinctions, his body no longer reacts with the sudden rush of fear that leads to flashbacks. Although Brian still experiences some flashbacks, their length and intensity have been reduced.

SELF AS CONTEXT

Another important aspect of ACT is learning to explore how we see ourselves using various descriptions. For example, we may think of ourselves as "strong" or "independent." We might also see ourselves as "a traumatized person" or "a damaged person." Our self-descriptions also involve the roles we play and what we do for a living. For example, we might use the word "mother" or "accountant" to portray ourselves. Acceptance and commitment therapy emphasizes learning to gain some distance from these descriptions. Although there are words to describe you, they are not the total essence of who you are. If you take a step back, you can actually notice the part of you that is doing the labeling. How does this apply to Brian? Brian has viewed himself as someone who has been damaged by war. By learning to view his thoughts without judgment and get some distance from them, he begins to recognize that he applies many labels to himself, including "husband," "soldier," and "strong." He also begins to appreciate that these are simply labels, and a part of him learns to observe the labeling—sort of like viewing labels being placed on a white envelope. Every time Brian thinks of himself as "a damaged person," he practices seeing it as just one label on the envelope. In time, he is able to see that there is part of him that can view the labels going on the envelope. He learns to watch the whole process, rather than getting upset by the content of each label. This technique helps him get some distance from the painful label of being "damaged."

EXPLORING VALUE AND ACTION

One very important aspect of ACT is its emphasis on helping you identify and commit to what you truly value in your life. We are all struggling to balance family, work, relationships, and, perhaps, spirituality. How we behave says a lot about what we truly value. By identifying what is important to you, you can start to figure out how you want to change your behavior. For example, when Brian considers his values, he realizes that being a veteran and serving his country are actually very important parts of his identity. Yet, because of his PTSD symptoms, he has avoided all contact with other veterans. Brian realizes that joining a support group will be a way for him to truly begin to identify with other veterans. After being involved in the group for several months, Brian finds himself taking a position of leadership. He begins to speak to soldiers with new war injuries. Although this is not the perfect life that Brian would have chosen for himself, he is learning how to act in accordance with his values of service and helping others. This is a key component of ACT.

The Common Elements of CBT, DBT, and ACT

Now that we have discussed each of these approaches, how can we tie them together? Recently, there has been a great interest in combining and integrating these treatments, because they share some common elements. For example, all three therapies place an emphasis on exposure to (versus avoidance of) your feelings and emotions. All the treatments also focus on practical problem-solving skills and on developing an awareness of your thoughts and emotions as they arise (Hoffman, Sayer, and Fang 2010). Mindfulness skills, found in both ACT and DBT approaches, may enhance traditional CBT therapy by helping you decrease your avoidance of trauma-related thoughts and feelings (Thompson, Arnkoff, and Glass 2011). Mindfulness can also increase your cognitive flexibility, which helps you see things from different viewpoints. That's a key skill in helping you bond with other people and feel a greater sense of interpersonal connection (Cukor et al. 2009; Follette, Palm, and Pearson 2006). Learning DBT skills might also help you prepare for CBT approaches (for example, exposure therapy) by reducing suicidal behaviors and improving your distress tolerance (Becker and Zayfert 2001). (However, if you are dealing with thoughts of suicide, it is very important that you not attempt the exercises in this book on your own. You should seek the help of a trained professional to help guide you.)

Basically, one size does not fit all in terms of trauma treatment. Gray and colleagues (2012) have found that certain aspects of exposure therapy can be enhanced by using techniques focused on your thoughts and exercises focused on living in line with what you truly value (compatible with ACT). Integrating these treatments and using specific techniques to target specific symptoms appears to hold great promise in PTSD treatment (Roemer and Orsillo 2009). For example, DBT appears to be very effective in reducing suicidal behavior and in helping people to manage their emotions (Linehan et al. 2006). And ACT appears to be effective in helping people to stop avoiding their emotions and get back in touch with their internal thoughts and feelings (Chawla and Ostafin 2007; Vujanovic et al. 2009).

Table 2 contains a brief summary of the techniques used in each therapy, allowing us to see at a glance what approaches they have in common.

Table 2: Summary of Techniques Used in CBT, DBT, and ACT

	CBT	DBT	ACT
Exposure Techniques	X	X	X
Interpersonal Skills	X	X	X
Behavioral Coping (for example, relaxation, breathing, and so on)	X	X	
Mindfulness		X	X
Cognitive Techniques	X	X	
Specific Discussion of Life Goals and Values			X
Distress Tolerance		X	X

How do you know which techniques are useful for you? Worksheet 6 will help you decide which CBT, DBT, and ACT techniques and exercises in the following chapters may be the most beneficial.

Worksheet 6: Which Techniques Are Right for Me?

Purpose: To help you decide which techniques will be most helpful for you.

Instructions: Mark the experiences below that apply to you. For yes answers, refer to the suggested worksheets.

	Check Your Answer	If You Answered Yes, Consider These Exercises
I struggle with nightmares of the traumatic event(s).	X No ___ Yes	CBT exposure techniques: worksheet 26
I have intrusive thoughts, images, flashbacks, or memories of the traumatic event(s) that affect my daily life.	___ No X Yes	CBT exposure techniques: worksheets 23 and 24 ACT techniques: worksheets 12 and 13
I struggle with thoughts of guilt and self-blame.	___ No X Yes	CBT techniques: worksheet 24 ACT techniques: worksheets 12 and 13
I avoid my thoughts, feelings, and emotions.	___ No X Yes	CBT techniques: worksheets 20 and 22 ACT and DBT techniques: worksheets 14 through 18
I have thoughts that upset me quite a bit.	___ No X Yes	CBT techniques: worksheets 11, 19, 22, and 23 ACT and DBT techniques: worksheets 12, 13, and 22
I have difficulty concentrating.	___ No X Yes	CBT techniques: worksheets 7, 8, and 9 ACT and DBT techniques: worksheets 12, 13, and 25

I am afraid my feelings about the traumatic event(s) will overwhelm me.	____ No _X_ Yes	ACT and DBT techniques: worksheets 14 through 18
I have difficulty connecting to other people.	____ No _X_ Yes	CBT techniques: worksheet 31 ACT and DBT techniques: worksheets 14, 15, 21, and 27
I have difficulty in identifying my emotions.	_X_ No ____ Yes	ACT and DBT techniques: worksheets 16, 17, and 18
I want to explore my larger values and goals in life.	____ No _X_ Yes	ACT techniques: worksheets 14 and 15
I experience a lot of physical symptoms—for example, my heart racing and palms sweating. CLENCHING	____ No _X_ Yes	CBT techniques: worksheets 8 and 9 DBT and ACT techniques: worksheets 12 and 13
I sometimes put myself down, and I'm very hard on myself.	____ No _X_ Yes	CBT techniques: worksheet 23 ACT and DBT techniques: worksheets 12, 13, and 24
I feel nervous, anxious, or tense most of the time.	____ No _X_ Yes	CBT techniques: worksheets 7 through 11 DBT and ACT techniques: worksheets 10 through 13, 25
I have thoughts of hurting myself or attempting suicide.	_X_ No ____ Yes	DBT techniques: worksheet 19, which should be completed with the help of a trained mental health professional

Conclusion

In recent years, there have been great advances in helping people who have survived trau-matic events. The therapies CBT, DBT, and ACT all have techniques that have been suc-cessful in the treatment of PTSD. Cognitive behavioral therapy (CBT) focuses on chang-ing thoughts and behaviors as a way to manage your emotions. The emphasis on exposure-based treatment helps you stop avoiding your trauma-related thoughts and mem-ories and feel a sense of mastery and control over your coping. Dialectical behavior therapy (DBT) and acceptance and commitment therapy (ACT) both bring the valuable practice of mindfulness into the picture. Learning to notice your environment and your internal states can be the first step in better managing your symptoms. Another technique from DBT and ACT is acceptance. We are always choosing whether to accept our emotions or work to change them. Both DBT and ACT emphasize that fighting to change your emo-tional state is not always the answer. Sometimes acceptance can actually lead to a calmer state of mind. The next three chapters focus on various types of PTSD symptoms and have exercises from all three of these therapies. You do not need to be diagnosed with PTSD to benefit from the exercises. By trying out some new things and finding what fits best for you, you can manage your symptoms and create a better life.

Chapter 4

Managing Your Anxiety

People who have experienced a traumatic event may find that they are tense, nervous, and anxious most of time. This is a very difficult way to live life. Anxiety can be overwhelming, and it can take a toll on both your emotional and your physical health. You may find yourself having difficulty falling or staying asleep. People with PTSD may also have difficulty concentrating, feel on edge much of the time, and be very easily startled. Finally, when you are anxious, you are prone to being irritable and angry, which is likely to take a toll on your relationships with other people.

Anxiety is a very strong emotion. When you are anxious, it is really difficult to participate in daily activities and almost impossible to enjoy life. For example, how can you experience joy in interacting with other people if all of your emotions are muted by anxiety? Think of it this way: if you are surrounded by the loud drilling of jackhammers every day, how can you possibly hear your favorite song playing on the radio? There are various ways to "turn down the volume" on your anxiety and start to participate in life more. Of course, no one strategy works for everyone—one size does not fit all. That is why this chapter contains many exercises for you to experiment with. These techniques have all been found to help people in general, but you are the expert on what will fit best into your life and work best for your particular situation. Each technique is presented in worksheet form; most of the worksheets are laid out so you can practice the technique for a week. You will probably want to make copies of the worksheets so you can practice over a period of weeks and months until these techniques become familiar and more automatic.

Building a Strong Foundation: Breathing

Every single anxiety management exercise has breathing at the core. This may sound overly simple—we all breathe instinctively in order to stay alive. But we rarely take time to focus on our breathing and understand its importance in our emotional and physical well being. Earlier in this book (in chapter 2) we discussed some basic relationships among thoughts, feelings, behavior, and physiology. All of these things influence each other. At first glance, it may seem very difficult to do anything to control your physiology. You may feel you have no control once your heart starts racing, you start sweating, your muscles are filled with tension, or your blood pressure goes up. In fact, hundreds of years ago, doctors and philosophers used to think there was no relation between what was going on in our minds and what was going on in our bodies. Now we know better. There is one very powerful tool we do have to manage our physiology, and that is our breath (Bourne 1995). Slowing down your breathing increases the amount of oxygen that goes to your muscles. It also helps to slow down your body systems, resulting in a decrease in heart rate, decreased muscle tension, and less sweating. In turn, these changes lead to your thoughts slowing down a little bit and your anxiety level being lowered. Perhaps this chain of events can help you to stay in a difficult situation rather than avoiding it because of anxiety.

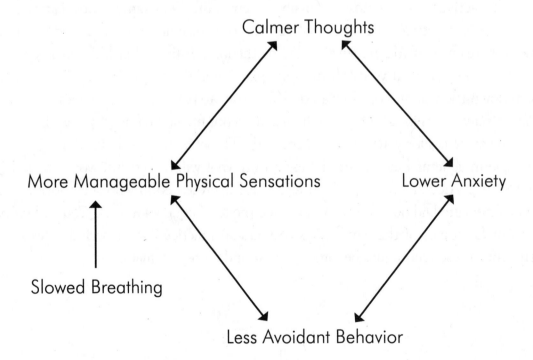

Figure 4: The Calming Effects of Slowed Breathing

Some Quick Tips Before You Practice Deep Breathing

Before you attempt to focus on your breath, you should know that it is important to let yourself make mistakes. It is not uncommon for people to feel self-conscious and worried prior to starting any type of relaxation exercises. If you feel nervous about the prospect of letting go, try to remember that you are in control of the process. Know also that it's normal to feel some anxiety when you first learn relaxation techniques. You can slowly build up your skills and the time you spend practicing. It's also important to remember that everyone feels strange at first. Most people are worried about how they look and may even feel silly when they first start focusing on their breath. Try to give yourself a place to practice where you feel relatively safe and comfortable. It's easier to learn a new skill in a quiet and calm environment, so don't try to master deep breathing during stressful times until you've practiced in calmer settings. If you practice these skills over weeks and months, you will begin to find that you pay attention to your breathing almost automatically. In summary:

- It is normal to be worried about letting go or to feel self-conscious.

- There is no such thing as the "perfect" breather!

- Practice in a calm environment so you can eventually use this skill in high-stress situations.

Worksheet 7: Focus on the Breath

Purpose: To help you learn and practice deep breathing skills. You may want to make photocopies of this worksheet and use one for each week you practice.

Instructions:

1. Choose a quiet place without distractions. If possible, choose an environment in which you feel fairly safe.

2. Place one hand on your belly and the other hand over your chest. Take a few regular breaths. You will probably notice that the hand on your chest moves up and down more than the one on your abdomen.

3. Now, as you take a breath, visualize filling your abdomen with air. See if you can make the hand over your abdomen rise and fall.

4. Now focus on slowing down your breathing. You can keep your eyes open or closed, whichever is comfortable for you. To time your breath, you can say the word the word "one" to yourself as you inhale and say the words "one-thousand" to yourself as you exhale. Do this for twenty counts ("one one-thousand" on the first breath, "two one-thousand" on the second breath, and so on). Pause. If you feel able, repeat for twenty more counts.

5. Remember, as you do this, that you don't have to be the "perfect" breather! Everyone's mind wanders from time to time. Everyone feels the need to fidget.

6. Log your practice below.

7. Before and after deep breathing, rate your level of anxiety on a scale of 0 to 10, where 0 is no anxiety at all and 10 is overwhelming anxiety.

Breathing Practice Day 1

Thoughts before deep breathing:

Level of anxiety before deep breathing: _____/10

Body sensations before deep breathing:

Thoughts after deep breathing:

Level of anxiety after deep breathing: _____/10

Body sensations after deep breathing:

Breathing Practice Day 2

Thoughts before deep breathing:

Level of anxiety before deep breathing: _____/10

Body sensations before deep breathing:

Thoughts after deep breathing:

Level of anxiety after deep breathing: _____/10

Body sensations after deep breathing:

Breathing Practice Day 3

Thoughts before deep breathing:

Level of anxiety before deep breathing: _____/10

Body sensations before deep breathing:

Thoughts after deep breathing:

Level of anxiety after deep breathing: _____/10

Body sensations after deep breathing:

Breathing Practice Day 4

Thoughts before deep breathing:

Level of anxiety before deep breathing: _____/10

Body sensations before deep breathing:

Thoughts after deep breathing:

Level of anxiety after deep breathing: _____/10

Body sensations after deep breathing:

Breathing Practice Day 5

Thoughts before deep breathing:

Level of anxiety before deep breathing: _____/10

Body sensations before deep breathing:

Thoughts after deep breathing:

Level of anxiety after deep breathing: _____/10

Body sensations after deep breathing:

Breathing Practice Day 6

Thoughts before deep breathing:

Level of anxiety before deep breathing: _____/10

Body sensations before deep breathing:

Thoughts after deep breathing:

Level of anxiety after deep breathing: _____/10

Body sensations after deep breathing:

Breathing Practice Day 7

Thoughts before deep breathing:

Level of anxiety before deep breathing: _____/10

Body sensations before deep breathing:

Thoughts after deep breathing:

Level of anxiety after deep breathing: _____/10

Body sensations after deep breathing:

Focusing on Your Body

Now that you have learned a very basic breathing technique, you can see what other types of relaxation and anxiety management skills appeal to you. Some people prefer to use their body when trying to decrease their anxiety levels, while other people have vivid imaginations and may find that their mind is their best relaxation tool. Try to see what works best with your routine, your life experiences, and your personality. The next exercise focuses on daily activity, which can help people manage negative emotions, including anxiety (Bertisch et al. 2009; Descilo et al. 2010).

Activity can take the form of exercise, stretching, or yoga, and is beneficial for many reasons. First of all, activity helps you get back in touch with and become more comfortable with your body. Second, activity helps you to *desensitize* to your body sensations. What does that mean? Right now, when your heart starts to race and you start to sweat, you probably immediately think you are in a state of anxiety or panic. Basically, your mind automatically connects these types of bodily reactions to anxiety. When you work out, however, sweating and increased heart rate are perfectly normal and expected reactions. Over time, your mind will start to associate these same bodily sensations with exercise. Eventually, you will not be as worried by sweaty palms or a racing heart, because when you exercise regularly, you learn that these sensations are manageable and not life-threatening (Barlow and Craske 2006).

When you start any kind of activity, it's important to ask your doctor what kind of activity is safe for you. Start with small, manageable goals. When making health-related changes, people tend to do better in the long run when they experience some success (Rollnick, Miller, and Butler 2008), so set goals you can meet! Ask yourself what is realistic (and perhaps even a little bit too easy) and start there. You can always increase your activity goals as you progress.

Worksheet 8: Getting Active

Purpose: To create a manageable goal and begin practicing an activity (stretching, yoga, exercise) on a regular basis.

Instructions: We'll start the worksheet with an example so you see how the sheet works. After that, set your goal and use the rest of the worksheet to record your activity sessions. You may photocopy this worksheet and use as needed.

Example:

My goal is to do some stretches and ten pushups for ten minutes each morning, three times this week.

Level of anxiety before activity: __6__ /10

Body sensations before activity: *I feel tired and my stomach feels "nervous."*

Level of anxiety after activity: __3__ /10

Body sensations after activity: *My arms feel sore (a good soreness). I feel less tired. My stomach feels fine.*

Exercise:

My goal is to _____ for _____ .
               (insert activity here)   (insert time frame here)

Activity Practice Session 1

Level of anxiety before activity: _____ /10

Body sensations before activity:

Level of anxiety after activity: _____ /10

Body sensations after activity:

Activity Practice Session 2

Level of anxiety before activity: _____/10

Body sensations before activity:

Level of anxiety after activity: _____/10

Body sensations after activity:

Activity Practice Session 3

Level of anxiety before activity: _____/10

Body sensations before activity:

Level of anxiety after activity: _____/10

Body sensations after activity:

Activity Practice Session 4

Level of anxiety before activity: _____/10

Body sensations before activity:

Level of anxiety after activity: _____/10

Body sensations after activity:

Activity Practice Session 5

Level of anxiety before activity: _____/10

Body sensations before activity:

Level of anxiety after activity: _____/10

Body sensations after activity:

Activity Practice Session 6

Level of anxiety before activity: _____/10

Body sensations before activity:

Level of anxiety after activity: _____/10

Body sensations after activity:

Activity Practice Session 7

Level of anxiety before activity: _____/10

Body sensations before activity:

Level of anxiety after activity: _____/10

Body sensations after activity:

In addition to regular activity, many people benefit from something called *progressive muscle relaxation*, or PMR for short. This is a set of exercises where you learn to tense and relax various muscle groups throughout your body. By learning the difference between the sensations of "tension" and "relaxation," you can learn to release tension as it is building up. For example, if you try to relieve soreness in your shoulders after your back and neck are extremely achy, it can be very difficult to do. However, if you can recognize when your shoulder blades are starting to inch up and the muscles in your neck are tightening, you can relax before your pain and stress levels are extremely high. As with the other exercises, it is important to practice PMR (worksheet 9) in a quiet environment. After weeks and months of practice, you will be able to use it in high-stress situations. Don't attempt to tense any muscle groups where doing so causes you pain. Consult with your doctor if you are unsure if this type of relaxation activity is right for you.

Worksheet 9: Progressive Muscle Relaxation

Purpose: To understand the difference between tension and relaxation in your body, so you can stop muscle tension before it builds up.

Instructions: Start in a comfortable position, sitting in a chair. Tense and relax each muscle group according to the guidance below. In each set of muscles, pay special attention to the difference between the feelings of tension and the feelings of relaxation. Hold each tense position for a count of ten. Release slowly and hold for ten seconds. Notice the differences in your muscles when tensed and when released. Rate your anxiety level before and after each practice session. Use a scale from 0 to 10, where 0 is no anxiety at all and 10 is overwhelming anxiety.

1. Tense your toes by curling them inward toward the soles of your feet. Release by letting them come back to their normal position.

2. Tense your ankles by bringing your toes up toward the ceiling while your heels stay on the ground. Release by letting them drop back to the floor.

3. Tense your calves and quadriceps (thigh) muscles by squeezing them. Release them completely.

4. Squeeze your gluteus muscles (the muscles of your buttocks) together. Release.

5. Tighten your stomach muscles by sucking your stomach in as far as you can. Release your stomach to its normal position.

6. Tense your back muscles by taking in a deep chest breath. Release as you exhale.

7. Tighten your shoulders and upper back by pushing your shoulder blades together. Release.

8. Tense your neck and shoulders by pushing your shoulders up toward your ears. Release as you let your shoulders droop to a comfortable position.

9. Clench your fists. Release by letting your fingers come back to a natural but somewhat curled position.

10. Tighten your biceps by extending your arms and "making a muscle." Release by letting your arms go.

11. Tense your forehead muscles by lifting your eyebrows up as far as they can go. Release.

12. Close your eyes until your face is "scrunched up," and feel the muscles around your eyes. Release and open your eyes.

13. Pucker your lips (an exaggerating "kissing" face). Relax as you let go of the muscles around your lips and jaw.

Example:

Level of anxiety before PMR: __8__/10

Level of anxiety after PMR: __4__/10

Notes on thoughts, feelings, and body sensations: *Before, I didn't even realize that I was tensing my shoulders most of the time. The difference between when they feel loose—way below my ears—and when I hold them up close to my chin is amazing. I feel a little bit nervous being this relaxed. My jaw still feels somewhat tight. I think I need to practice with this muscle group.*

Exercise:

PMR Practice Session 1

Level of anxiety before PMR: _____/10

Level of anxiety after PMR: _____/10

Notes on thoughts, feelings, and body sensations:

PMR Practice Session 2

Level of anxiety before PMR: _____/10

Level of anxiety after PMR: _____/10

Notes on thoughts, feelings, and body sensations:

PMR Practice Session 3

Level of anxiety before PMR: _____/10

Level of anxiety after PMR: _____/10

Notes on thoughts, feelings, and body sensations:

PMR Practice Session 4

Level of anxiety before PMR: _____/10

Level of anxiety after PMR: _____/10

Notes on thoughts, feelings, and body sensations:

PMR Practice Session 5

Level of anxiety before PMR: _____/10

Level of anxiety after PMR: _____/10

Notes on thoughts, feelings, and body sensations:

PMR Practice Session 6

Level of anxiety before PMR: _____/10

Level of anxiety after PMR: _____/10

Notes on thoughts, feelings, and body sensations:

PMR Practice Session 7

Level of anxiety before PMR: _____/10

Level of anxiety after PMR: _____/10

Notes on thoughts, feelings, and body sensations:

Using Your Mind to Relax and Develop Awareness

The next set of exercises focus on how your mind can help you manage anxiety. Some people have great imaginations and pay a lot of attention to little details. Even if you don't think you are one of those people, try some of these exercises a few times. You may find you improve a lot with a few practice sessions. You can use these skills for two purposes. First, you can distract yourself from stressful and anxiety-provoking situations by thinking about something more pleasant. Second, you can use some of these skills to ground yourself when you feel high levels of anxiety or panic. Grounding helps you to come back to the present moment by paying attention to your current surroundings. Many CBT exercises are focused on using thoughts and activities as a way to distract yourself from feelings of anxiety. In contrast, ACT and DBT exercises are focused on noticing, observing, and accepting thoughts, feelings, and sensations rather than struggling to change them. This is some-times called "grounding yourself in the present moment." Experimenting with various exercises in this section will help you decide which approach works best for you.

Imagery and Grounding Exercises

The following exercise (worksheet 10) is focused on different types of imagery. Because everyone is different, there are several options for each of your five senses. These exercises are just a guideline. If you find any exercise upsetting, discontinue it and try something else. Feel free to experiment to find what works for you.

Worksheet 10: Engaging the Senses

Purpose: To practice using various types of imagery (sight, sound, smell, touch, taste) in order to 1) develop a longer imagery script based on your results, and 2) set a specific goal involving sensory awareness in your daily life.

Instructions: There are ten exercises below. Read through each one slowly and try to imagine each scene. Complete the questions afterward to determine which type of imagery suits you the best.

Sight Exercise 1: Imagine yourself in front of a large green tree. As you walk closer to the tree, you pick up one of its thick, waxy leaves. You see the veins on the leaf making a beautiful, symmetrical pattern. As you look at the tree, you notice that the leaves vary in color—from a deep, bright emerald to a pale, faded yellow.

Sight Exercise 2: Imagine you are on a sandy brown beach. As you walk to the shore, you see the sand getting darker and darker as it is soaked with water from the ocean. The water is clear and bright. As you look toward the horizon, there is water as far as the eye can see. The bright blue water meets the pale blue sky as you look out and see the bright orange sunlight.

Sound Exercise 1: You are in a beautiful park. As you walk along, you see a gorgeous waterfall, and you concentrate on the sound of the water rushing over the rocks. You can hear the sound of birds chirping. As you return from your walk, you begin to hum your favorite song. You can hear the tune in your head—the words, the instruments. You are enjoying the sounds of your walk.

Sound Exercise 2: As you walk among the trees, you hear the sound of the wind rustling gently. As you stop, you hear the faraway sound of a squirrel running through crunchy, dry leaves. Then, it is completely quiet. You hear the ticking of your watch and the quiet sound of your breath as you inhale and exhale.

Touch Exercise 1: You are on the beach and see a beautiful sea shell. You pick it up and notice its edges are perfectly ridged. You rub your fingers over the shell and appreciate the bumpy edges and glossy smooth interior. You pick up a handful of sand and run it through your fingers. It feels hot and fine and slips easily though your fingers.

Touch Exercise 2: You get up in the morning and dip your hands in a basin of cool water. Your hands feel light and buoyant as they are under the water. You splash the cool water on your face. Your feel the drops of refreshing water drip down your eyelashes and temples. You feel a soft towel on your face; it feels lush and warm. The cool air from the nearby fan blows on your cheeks, and you feel refreshed.

Taste Exercise 1: You have a large plate of homemade chocolate chip cookies in front of you. As you bite into a cookie, you can taste the delicious buttery flavor and the sweet chocolate chips. The cookie is just out of the oven, so it is soft and melts in your mouth. You enjoy each bite of the cookie.

Taste Exercise 2: You pour yourself a large glass of cold lemonade. The lemons have been freshly squeezed, and there is very little sugar in your drink. It is tart and tangy as it hits the inside of your mouth. The lemonade tastes refreshing and delicious.

Smell Exercise 1: You are baking a tray of chocolate chip cookies. You look in the oven and see they are almost done. You can smell the sugary dough and the chocolate. As you inhale, you feel the aroma go all the way through your nose and down into your hungry stomach.

Smell Exercise 2: You are walking in a beautiful garden of roses. You can smell the floral sweetness. Nearby you see some beautiful lilacs. As you inhale, you notice the difference between the bold scent of rose and the delicate scent of the lilacs.

Questions

1. Which exercise was the easiest for you? Which one felt the most real?

_____

_____

2. Which exercise was the most difficult?

_____

_____

Use your answers to questions 1 and 2 to identify which senses are easiest for you to imagine using.

Distraction Exercise

Now write a longer imagery script for yourself, using whichever of the senses were easiest to imagine.

Read the script to yourself once a day for two weeks. In time you will be able to use these images to distract you when you feel extremely anxious. For example, if you respond to feelings of touch and sound, you might write a description of your last beach vacation that includes details about the feel of the sand and water and the sound of the sea gulls.

_____

_____

_____

_____

_____

_____

_____

_____

Grounding Exercise

Using the senses that are easy for you to imagine, choose specific senses to focus on in your daily activities. Set a specific goal.

Example (using touch and smell): I will practice noticing the feel of the warm water and smelling the scent of the dish soap when I do the dishes after dinner this week.

Exercise:

I will practice _____ for/during _____ .
                   (specific activity)   (specified duration)

Now that you have some experience with using your five senses and your imagination, you can experiment with coming up with various ways to use imagery in your daily life. Try to pay attention to details in your surroundings. Focus on whatever senses are easiest for you, noticing sights, sounds, feel, tastes, or smells. Take a few minutes every day to use these skills. You can pay attention to your actual environment or you can create a detailed imaginary scene that you find calming and restful. Either way, sustained practice will help lower your overall level of anxiety.

Decreasing the Power of Negative Thoughts

There is one more important way that your mind influences your overall anxiety level. Your thoughts can be helpful or harmful in your effort to overcome PTSD and other effects of trauma. It's likely that you have very negative and painful thoughts about yourself, the actual traumatic event(s) you've lived through, and your future. Most survivors experience thoughts that can greatly increase their overall level of anxiety and worry. For example, you might think that you are somehow to blame for what happened to you, or you might believe that there was something about you that invited victimization. You might also believe that traumatic things will keep happening to you and that you will never be able to heal from what you've experienced.

It can help to think of these thoughts as completely natural and normal. From a CBT perspective, you can consider finding other ways to look at these thoughts. From an ACT perspective, these thoughts do not need to be judged or evaluated at all. Simply learning to observe them and let them be may provide you with relief.

The first step to making these thoughts less powerful is to pay attention and notice when you are having them. For the second step, you have two options. Using option one (based on a CBT approach), once you identify these thoughts, you can work to replace them with more helpful, less painful ways of viewing the situation. This doesn't mean you have to put on rose-colored glasses or be unrealistically positive about life. It means that you try to look at a situation more realistically and consider other possibilities. Worksheet 11 (below) contains examples of how to do this. For example, if you have the thought "Things will never get better for someone like me," you could tell yourself, "I have no way of knowing what the future holds. I do have small moments of happiness these days. Maybe if I keep working on my goals, those moments will happen more often." When you look at the situation in an alternative way, your emotions may feel more manageable and less intense.

Option two (based on ACT and DBT techniques) involves simply observing your thoughts, without getting involved in the particular content. This approach is not about changing what you believe. It is about learning how to observe what is going on in your mind without judgment. For example, if you have the thought "Things will never get better for someone like me," you could tell yourself, "Many people with PTSD have thoughts like this. This is just a thought. It doesn't have to define me." This approach takes some practice, but it can be very useful in the long run. Eventually, you might come to see these thoughts as fleeting and unimportant events—like spam e-mail that can simply be deleted. Worksheets 12 and 13 outline this approach of taking a more detached, nonjudgmental view of your thoughts. Both these techniques can help you to break the link between your thoughts (in this case negative thoughts about yourself, what happened to you, and your future) and your emotions (in this case anxiety).

Changing Negative and Painful Thoughts

The next exercise (worksheet 11) is based on the CBT approach of identifying and challenging your negative and painful thoughts. You may find that this is a technique that works well for you.

Worksheet 11: Observing and Changing Anxiety Thoughts

Purpose: To learn how to identify painful thoughts and replace them with more balanced, helpful alternatives.

Instructions: Use the worksheet to monitor any anxiety or worry-related thoughts you have for a period of one week and to come up with alternative ways to view these situations. When rating your emotions, use a scale from 0 to 10, where 0 is none at all and 10 is overwhelming.

Example:

Thought: *I am a bad person. Things will keep going wrong for me.*

Emotions: *Guilt and fear*

Intensity level: *10/10*

Alternative thought: *I have had some difficult things happen to me. I didn't deserve them. Other people tell me I am a good person. Maybe they are seeing something I don't right now.*

Emotions: Relief

Intensity level: *4/10*

Exercise:

Day 1 Practice

Thought:

Emotions:

Intensity level: _____/10

Alternative thought:

Emotions:

Intensity level: _____/10

Day 2 Practice

Thought:

Emotions:

Intensity level: _____/10

Alternative thought:

Emotions:

Intensity level: _____/10

Day 3 Practice

Thought:

Emotions:

Intensity level: _____/10

Alternative thought:

Emotions:

Intensity level: _____/10

Day 4 Practice

Thought:

Emotions:

Intensity level: _____/10

Alternative thought:

Emotions:

Intensity level: _____/10

Day 5 Practice

Thought:

Emotions:

Intensity level: _____/10

Alternative thought:

Emotions:

Intensity level: _____/10

Day 6 Practice

Thought:

Emotions:

Intensity level: _____/10

Alternative thought:

Emotions:

Intensity level: _____/10

Day 7 Practice:

Thought:

Emotions:

Intensity level: _____/10

Alternative thought:

Emotions:

Intensity level: _____ /10

Observing and Accepting Painful Thoughts

Sometimes you can't change the content of your thoughts, no matter how hard you try. Perhaps there is some truth to what you are telling yourself. For example, you may think, "I drank so much that I couldn't take care of myself that night." Of course, no one should ever hurt you when you are in that condition! But the healthy alternative thought, "No one should have hurt me, regardless of how much alcohol I drank," may be difficult for you believe. In this case, it is easier to observe your thoughts and use the word "and" in between them, rather than deciding which one is the more true. So, as you observe your thoughts, add the healthy alternative rather than revise the existing thought: "I should not have drunk so much that night AND no one had the right to hurt me." This approach can also be powerful if you have guilt about things you did or didn't do during the traumatic event (Steenkamp et al. 2011). For example, in combat, domestic violence, and other high-stress situations, people face horrible dilemmas. Perhaps you have done things you are not proud of. Perhaps other people were hurt as a result of some of the decisions you made. Again, rather than trying to change these beliefs, try observing them and using the word "and" in between the thoughts.

The next exercise (worksheet 12) focuses on simply observing your thoughts. The purpose of this type of exercise is to help you develop some emotional distance from your own thoughts, which helps to reduce your anxiety, worry, and emotional pain. This type of approach definitely takes practice. It is interesting that experienced meditators (like Christian and Buddhist monks) are well-practiced in viewing their thoughts in this way (Lutz et al. 2008). Worksheet 12 has several metaphors for you to choose from. Make sure you pick an image that is relaxing and calm for you. You shouldn't pick any metaphors that remind you of your traumatic experience(s).

Worksheet 12: Observing Painful Thoughts

Purpose: To learn how to observe your thoughts without judgment.

Instructions:

1. Choose a quiet place without distractions. If possible, choose an environment where you feel fairly safe.

2. Sit in a comfortable chair. Your eyes can be open or closed, whichever is comfortable. Set a timer for 4 minutes.

3. Notice the thoughts that come and go in your mind. You do not need to figure out if the thoughts are true or false, or to think about what they mean. Just observe them. Choose a metaphor about the thoughts and their passing that works well for you, such as:

    a. You are on a cloud. It is soft and comfortable. Imagine that all the thoughts you have are on other clouds in the sky. You can watch them float by you. Just observe them. Watch them come and go. You do not need to get involved in the particular content of any thought—you are safe on your cloud.

    b. Imagine you are seated comfortably and your thoughts are running on a conveyor belt in front of you. You are not in control of the speed of the conveyor. If you are tempted to look into the boxes, just pull out a label and write the word "thought" on it. You can put the label on the box and watch it go down the conveyor belt.

    c. You are sitting on the beach in a comfortable chair. Your thoughts are like waves. You watch them roll in and out on the shore. Your feet are firmly in the sand. Some waves are gentle and pause as they hug the shore. Then they recede. Some waves are strong and forceful as the come up on the shore. These waves recede quickly. You can just observe the various waves as you are seated safely on the shore.

    d. You are in an airplane that is cruising at a high altitude. It is a very smooth ride. As you look below, you notice small houses and roads. You can see cars making their way on meandering roads. As the thoughts come and go in your mind, you notice them in the same way you notice the houses and cars you see in the distance. They will stay in your mind for a while and then they will pass out of view.

4. Log your practice below. To rate your anxiety level, use a scale from 0 to 10, where 0 is no anxiety at all and 10 is overwhelming anxiety. Body sensations include how your body is feeling—for example, your heart racing, sweaty palms, tension in your muscles, or a stomach or headache. This worksheet has space for seven days of thought observation; you may photocopy it to use over a longer period.

Thought Observation Day 1

Level of anxiety before thought observation: _____/10

Body sensations before thought observation:

Level of anxiety after thought observation: _____/10

Body sensations after thought observation:

Thought Observation Day 2

Level of anxiety before thought observation: _____/10

Body sensations before thought observation:

Level of anxiety after thought observation: _____/10

Body sensations after thought observation:

Thought Observation Day 3

Level of anxiety before thought observation: _____/10

Body sensations before thought observation:

Level of anxiety after thought observation: _____/10

Body sensations after thought observation:

Thought Observation Day 4

Level of anxiety before thought observation: _____/10

Body sensations before thought observation:

Level of anxiety after thought observation: _____/10

Body sensations after thought observation:

Thought Observation Day 5

Level of anxiety before thought observation: _____/10

Body sensations before thought observation:

Level of anxiety after thought observation: _____/10

Body sensations after thought observation:

Thought Observation Day 6

Level of anxiety before thought observation: _____/10

Body sensations before thought observation:

Level of anxiety after thought observation: _____/10

Body sensations after thought observation:

Thought Observation Day 7

Level of anxiety before thought observation: _____/10

Body sensations before thought observation:

Level of anxiety after thought observation: _____/10

Body sensations after thought observation:

Getting some distance from your thoughts and emotions can help you realize that you are more than just the contents of your mind and the sensations in your body (Hayes, Strosahl, and Wilson 1999). It is difficult to realize that there is part of you that exists outside of this, and the idea that there is might sound pretty metaphysical and "out there." But take a step back and consider. When you have a thought, part of you is experiencing that thought, but part of you is actually observing that you are having a thought. Similarly, when you feel something in your body, part of you is observing what you are feeling. The technique given in worksheet 13 (which has some similarities to the one in worksheet 12) helps you to realize that thoughts and emotions, regardless of whether they are positive or negative, are only a part of your true self (Hayes, Strosahl, and Wilson 1999). People have all sorts of names for this aspect of themselves—their true self, their soul, their essence, their spirit. Thinking too much about this concept probably won't help you to see if it is right for you. After some practice, you will be able to see if it helps you.

Worksheet 13: Observing Thoughts and Emotions

Purpose: To learn how to get some distance from your thoughts and emotions.

Instructions:

1. Choose a quiet place without distractions. If possible, try to choose an environment in which you feel fairly safe.

2. Sit in a comfortable chair. Your eyes can be open or closed, whichever is comfortable. Set a timer for 4 minutes.

3. Think about where you are now. Focus on the sensations of your body and the thoughts going through your mind. How do you feel? Notice if you feel calm, relaxed, anxious, irritated, and so on. As you do this, notice that there is a part of you that actually is the observer: this is the part of you that is able to put words to what is going on. Notice how the observer is observing the actual experience of what is going on in your mind and body.

4. Now think about a time when you felt really happy. Think about what was going on. Who was there? What were your feelings? What was going on in your body? Notice that there was a part of you that was observing or noticing what was going on. That is the same part of you that was present just a moment ago. That is present now.

5. Now think about a time when you felt irritated or upset. Think about what was going on. Who was there? What were your feelings? What was going on in your body? Notice that there was a part of you that was observing or noticing what was going on. This is the same part of you that was present just a moment ago. That is present now.

6. Take a moment to notice that "observer" part of yourself. Try to breathe and simply allow yourself to notice your thoughts and feelings. You do not need to push away any thoughts or feelings. Simply allow yourself to observe what is going on.

7. Log your practice below. This worksheet has space for seven days of thought and feeling observation; you may photocopy it to use over a longer period.

Observation Day 1

Notes on my thoughts, body sensations, and feelings before and after practice:

Observation Day 2

Notes on my thoughts, body sensations, and feelings before and after practice:

Observation Day 3

Notes on my thoughts, body sensations, and feelings before and after practice:

Observation Day 4

Notes on my thoughts, body sensations, and feelings before and after practice:

Observation Day 5

Notes on my thoughts, body sensations, and feelings before and after practice:

Observation Day 6

Notes on my thoughts, body sensations, and feelings before and after practice:

Observation Day 7

Notes on my thoughts, body sensations, and feelings before and after practice:

Conclusion

Many people who have experienced traumatic events feel anxious and worried most of the time, which is a really terrible way to live. Anxiety takes a toll on your body and your mind. Luckily, there are ways to break the cycle between your anxious thoughts, your body's reactions, and your emotions. Some of these techniques involve calming your body, and others involve changing or just observing your thoughts. All of the techniques share a focus on relaxed, deep breathing. The more you practice these techniques, the more they can help you participate in and enjoy life. If you practice regularly, you will also be able to use them in times of high stress. It's okay if you have trouble with these exercises at first. Experiment with what you like, and feel free to change the exercises to fit with your routine and personality. The key is to practice over weeks and months. Retraining your anxious body and mind takes a while, but it's a key step in healing.

Chapter 5

Stop Avoiding and Start Living Again

Many people who have lived through trauma avoid things that remind them of what they've been through. Certainly, avoidance is a key feature of PTSD. You may find yourself going to great lengths to avoid thoughts, feelings, people, and places that remind you of the traumatic event or events. As we discussed in chapter 2, although avoidance can work in the short term, in the long term, it usually breaks down. You may find yourself living a very limited life with a very restricted comfort zone. Eventually, avoidance can be debilitating.

It is natural to try to avoid painful feelings, but this type of coping can be taken to an extreme. If you push away emotions constantly, you might actually have difficulty figuring out what feelings and emotions you are experiencing (Linehan 1993). People with PTSD sometimes say they don't even have the words to describe what they are feeling; it's the psychological equivalent of being numb. You may also find you cannot recall many of your trauma-related memories. On the surface, this may seem okay. But when you dig deeper, you might realize that your lack of memories makes you feel dazed, confused, and disoriented. You might also find yourself feeling detached and withdrawn from other people and avoiding activities that you used to enjoy. This lack of connection can be extremely upsetting for people with PTSD. Finally, PTSD can cause you to feel you may not live as long as other people—that your future will somehow be cut short—for example, you might not expect to live past a certain age or you might think that you won't experience milestones in life (like getting married or having children). This is understandable if you've lived through something horrible. Part of healing is to find ways to process what has happened to you and learn to have hope for your future.

Finding Your Own Motivation

Tackling avoidance is not an easy thing to do. It takes a lot of courage to start doing things that may be uncomfortable for you. One way to get motivated in this process is to take a look at how PTSD is limiting your life and getting in the way of your longer-term goals. Worksheet 14 provides a place to start.

Worksheet 14: The Effects of PTSD on Values and Goals

Purpose: To understand how PTSD has limited your life and develop motivation to make changes.

Instructions: First, write a few sentences about how your symptoms interfere with your ability to interact with your family, hold a job, connect with friends, or develop a sense of spirituality (see the example just below). Second, rate how important each of the several aspects of your life is to you (family, work, and so on), and how satisfying it is. Third, use this information to come up with an important aspect of life that has been affected by your symptoms and that you want to improve. Finally, come up with three goals to pursue in the short term that will improve that aspect (see the example).

Example:

Because of what happened to me in the military, I have a really difficult time connecting with other people. I spend a lot of time crying and feeling overwhelmed. I don't want my kids to see how upset I am most of the time. They don't know about what happened to me. I don't talk about it. My relationship with my daughters has really suffered—I know they don't feel close to me. I don't go to church anymore—I don't know if ever will.

Family:

____ Not Important   ____ Somewhat Important   _X_ Very Important

_X_ Not Satisfied   ____ Somewhat Satisfied   ____ Very Satisfied

Work:

____ Not Important   _X_ Somewhat Important   ____ Very Important

____ Not Satisfied   _X_ Somewhat Satisfied   ____ Very Satisfied

Relationships:

____ Not Important   ____ Somewhat Important   _X_ Very Important

____ Not Satisfied   _X_ Somewhat Satisfied   ____ Very Satisfied

Spirituality:

____ Not Important   _X_ Somewhat Important   ____ Very Important

_X_ Not Satisfied   ____ Somewhat Satisfied   ____ Very Satisfied

Area of Focus: *Family*

Goals:

   a. *Take my kids to the movies once a month even though I might feel nervous about it.*

   b. *Have lunch with my mom and tell her that I still sometimes think a lot about my experiences in the military. (I'm going to tell her that I don't want to go into the details of my experiences right now, but that I wanted her to know.)*

   c. *Play a board game with my daughters once a week, on Sunday mornings. I haven't done this in a long, long time. Let my girls choose which game to play.*

Exercise:

1. Ways my symptoms interfere with important aspects of my life:

2. Rate the importance of each of the following aspects of your life, and your satisfaction with them.

Family:

____ Not Important   ____ Somewhat Important   ____ Very Important

____ Not Satisfied   ____ Somewhat Satisfied   ____ Very Satisfied

Work:

____ Not Important   ____ Somewhat Important   ____ Very Important

____ Not Satisfied   ____ Somewhat Satisfied   ____ Very Satisfied

Relationships:

____ Not Important   ____ Somewhat Important   ____ Very Important

____ Not Satisfied   ____ Somewhat Satisfied   ____ Very Satisfied

Spirituality:

____ Not Important   ____ Somewhat Important   ____ Very Important

____ Not Satisfied   ____ Somewhat Satisfied   ____ Very Satisfied

3. Now look at your ratings above and choose the area that is the most important to you AND that you are least satisfied with. Basically, choose one area to start working on.

Area of Focus:

4. Now list three specific, small goals you want to achieve in the next three months.

    a.

    b.

    c.

Using Metaphors to Help Bring about Change

Now that you have identified some of your key motivating factors and set some goals, it is useful to think about how you are going to get ready to actually make some changes. One technique involves the use of metaphors. These can help give you a different framework for thinking about your symptoms, which can help you think about your situation with less avoidance.

Worksheet 15: Creating a Change Metaphor

Purpose: To create your own change metaphor, allowing you to get a different perspective on your trauma-related thoughts and encouraging you to face difficult situations and emotions. You can create metaphors that emphasize your willingness to experience difficult emotions, and metaphors that emphasize changing and controlling your situation. Experiment with metaphors to find one that works for you.

Instructions: Read the examples below. Then create your own metaphor for facing the particular PTSD-related situations, thoughts, and feelings you avoid. If you are having trouble getting started, think of an activity, thing, or place that you love or find inspiring and use that to shape the creation of the metaphor.

Example 1:

My change metaphor is a garden. I think I need to look at my life like a garden. I would have loved a yard full of roses and plenty of vegetable plants. But I know that most of my yard is too shady and not rainy enough to raise lettuce. I am going to accept the garden I have, where I notice the green hostas growing well and a few yellow dandelions on the edges.

Example 2:

My change metaphor is my living room. I really hate the color brown, but most of the furniture and the walls of my living room are brown. I totally avoid my living room. The shape of the room is all wrong too—it's too long and narrow, so it's hard to fit in the sofa I want. I never read books in there and rarely sit there to relax. Recently, I realized that avoiding that room doesn't make it any less brown and it doesn't change the shape—it just means I have less space to hang out. I'm going to start figuring out how to redo that room to make it a place that I can use. I guess that means opening the door to that brown room and figuring out what I want to do next.

Example 3:

My change metaphor is a desert island. I feel like I am on a desert island and the only way to get back to civilization is to use a small boat to row back to the mainland. I know the waters are choppy and scary, but I'm going to keep my goal in mind. It will be an uncertain journey, but the destination is worth the trip. I'm going to make this journey.

Exercise:

My change metaphor is

Facing Your Emotions

It will take practice over months to get back in touch with your emotions, particularly if you feel emotionally numb or have become skilled at avoiding what you are feeling. The first step in facing your emotions is to begin to identify them. The next exercise, in worksheet 16, focuses on finding words that will be helpful for expressing your feelings. In worksheet 17, then, you'll start putting these words to work.

Worksheet 16: Identifying Emotions

Purpose: To increase your emotional vocabulary so that you can get back in touch with your emotions.

Instructions: Read the lists below; if you like, try to add your own words to them.

Words Related to Love	Words Related to Joy	Words Related to Surprise	Words Related to Sadness	Words Related to Anger	Words Related to Fear
Adoring	Happy	Amazed	Unhappy	Enraged	Anxious
Fond	Elated	Astonished	Hopeless	Furious	Nervous
Affectionate	Blissful	Astounded	Wistful	Fuming	Tense
Warm	Delighted	Dazed	Pensive	Livid	Confused
Compassionate	Cheerful	Speechless	Despondent	Irate	Worried
Sympathetic	Hopeful	Shocked	Disappointed	Upset	Edgy
Passionate	Optimistic	Flabbergasted	Miserable	Distraught	Panicky
Infatuated	Upbeat		Overwhelmed	Mad	Uneasy
Sentimental	Confident		Aggrieved	Bothered	Apprehensive
Touched	Satisfied		Hurt	Annoyed	Horrified
Tender	Comfortable		Disturbed		
	Calm		Inconsolable		
	Peaceful		Guilty		
	Content		Ashamed		
	Serene		Mortified		
	Pleased		Embarrassed		
	Encouraged		Reflective		
	Thrilled		Exhausted		
	Excited		Mournful		
			Regretful		

Clearly, there are many, many words to describe what a person might be feeling. The next step is to practice using these words to label what you yourself are feeling. In worksheet 17 you will find a template for emotion diary cards to use for practice. Make copies of the page and cut the copies into cards so you can fill out cards for several weeks. The easiest way to remember to fill out the cards is to tie them to things you do every day—do one when you are eating lunch, before you pick your kids up from school, or after your favorite TV show. Or simply set a cell phone alarm to remind you.

Worksheet 17: Emotion Diary Cards

Purpose: To notice and label what you are feeling. Refer to worksheet 16 if you have trouble coming up with labels. The point of this exercise is not to change your emotions, just to notice them.

Instructions: Fill out a card three times a day, using a few words to capture what you are feeling. Photocopy this page to create as many cards as you need.

Emotions	**Emotions**	**Emotions**
Date:	Date:	Date:
Time 1:	Time 1:	Time 1:
Time 2:	Time 2:	Time 2:
Time 3:	Time 3:	Time 3:
Emotions	**Emotions**	**Emotions**
Date:	Date:	Date:
Time 1:	Time 1:	Time 1:
Time 2:	Time 2:	Time 2:
Time 3:	Time 3:	Time 3:
Emotions	**Emotions**	**Emotions**
Date:	Date:	Date:
Time 1:	Time 1:	Time 1:
Time 2:	Time 2:	Time 2:
Time 3:	Time 3:	Time 3:

Developing Mindfulness

Another way to learn to identify and manage your emotions is to develop mindfulness—that is, to work to become aware of the present moment. This means letting yourself be aware of what is going on without judgment. Mindfulness is not about changing your emotions. Often, when we try to push negative thoughts and emotions away, they come back even stronger. When we don't try to push them away, emotions tend to be like waves. They tend to come in, wash up on the beach, and then recede. You can think of yourself as a surfer, riding the waves of emotion as they rise and fall. Mindfulness is all about how to appreciate your thoughts and emotions as waves. Learning mindfulness takes a lot of practice, but you don't need to be meditating or praying to master it. There are many everyday situations that present a perfect opportunity to practice mindfulness (Kabat-Zinn 1994). Worksheet 18 will help you practice everyday mindfulness.

Worksheet 18: Everyday Mindfulness Exercises

Purpose: To practice mindfulness in everyday life so that you begin to feel more connected to the present moment.

Instructions: Do these exercises as often as possible over the course of the next month. Attempt to do at least one a day. You can make multiple photocopies of these two pages so that you can use them again and again.

Exercise	What You Observed (Include as Many Senses as You Can in the Description)	Were You Able to Stay in the Present Moment?
Example: Peeling and eating an orange	*I noticed the thick rind of the orange stuck under my fingernails. I felt the bumpy texture and noticed the very vibrant orange color. The smell was sharp and almost acidic. It tasted sweet and the skin of the sections was chewy.*	____ No, I was very easily distracted. _X_ No, my mind wandered a few times. ____ Yes, I was able to stay mostly in the moment. ____ Yes, I was able to focus and concentrate on this experience.
When you are walking around your house or up the stairs, notice the movements of your body. Purposefully slow down. Pay attention to the movements of your muscles, your breath, and the sights and sounds around you.		____ No, I was very easily distracted. ____ No, my mind wandered a few times. ____ Yes, I was able to stay mostly in the moment. ____ Yes, I was able to focus and concentrate on this experience.

When you are washing the dishes, pay attention to all the sensations—for example, the feeling of the water and the smell of the soap.		____ No, I was very easily distracted. ____ No, my mind wandered a few times. ____ Yes, I was able to stay mostly in the moment. ____ Yes, I was able to focus and concentrate on this experience.
Eat an entire meal without reading, watching television, or talking. Pay attention to the sights, sounds, smells, textures, and flavors of the food.		____ No, I was very easily distracted. ____ No, my mind wandered a few times. ____ Yes, I was able to stay mostly in the moment. ____ Yes, I was able to focus and concentrate on this experience.

Handling Difficult Thoughts

This may sound strange, but we talk to ourselves more than anyone else in the course of a day. We are constantly saying things to ourselves in our minds. These thoughts can help motivate us, but they can also keep us stuck in unhealthy patterns. Most people with PTSD struggle with difficult thoughts that can keep them stuck. There are two main therapeutic approaches for handling these types of thoughts. One is to try to identify them and change them (which is the CBT approach we will discuss here) and the other is to just notice those thoughts and let them come and go without taking them literally or acting on them (which is an approach we discussed in chapter 4).

There are some really common ways that we tend to think, ways that can actually make our emotional pain worse. Here are some examples of those thinking styles and healthier alternatives (Burns 1999).

1. *All or nothing thinking.* Maybe you have difficulty seeing the gray areas in things. This is particularly difficult for people with PTSD. For example, you may think to yourself, "I will never be the same person I was before the trauma." A healthier thought might be, "Although I am definitely changed, there are aspects of me that are still the same."

2. *Overgeneralization.* This is when you decide that some event or situation is more common than it is, based on one or very few instances of the event. For example: "I was raped by a man, so I can never trust any man ever again." A healthier alternative: "I know that trust is difficult for me, but perhaps there are a few people out there whom I could trust, if I got to know them over time."

3. *Should statements.* These are related to overgeneralization. Should statements are overgeneralizations in which we decide something should be a certain way, and we get stuck in this way of thinking. For example: "Bad things shouldn't happen to good people." A healthier alternative: "Sometimes things are unfair, and bad things do happen to good people. Instead of getting stuck in the unfairness, I am not going to let this event define the rest of my life."

4. *Personalization.* This happens when we assume that we have a role in causing certain events (including other people's behavior) even though we have no evidence to support the assumption. For example: "She must not want me around her kids because she assumes I'm an angry veteran." A healthier alternative: "I don't know what is motivating her right now. Who knows what is happening in her life?"

5. *Filtering.* This is when you might concentrate only on certain aspects of a situation and ignore others. For example: "I felt like no one at the party understood what I've been though." A healthier alternative is: "It's hard for me to connect with other people. I do appreciate that my neighbor tried to talk to me about my military service—I know she has no idea what I lived through."

6. *Jumping to conclusions.* You may find yourself deciding you know the outcome of a situation when you have no evidence. For example: "I know exposure treatments won't work for me. There's no way I could talk about this stuff again." A healthier alternative: "I know this is going to be one of the hardest things I've ever tried. I suppose if it is too much for me, I can stop. But I won't know unless I attempt it."

7. *Catastrophizing.* When you have decided that the worst possible outcome is definitely going to happen, you are catastrophizing. For example: "I have nightmares every night. There is no way I am ever going to sleep again, and I'm surely going to die from this stress." A healthier alternative: "I am struggling with sleep right now, but this is a normal reaction to what I've been through. I will keep working to find solutions to this."

Worksheet 19: Managing Difficult Thoughts

Purpose: To learn how to identify and challenge difficult thoughts.

Instructions: Over the next week, write down your distressing thoughts twice a day. Identify the emotions that you are feeling. (Use worksheet 16 if you need help finding the right words.) Try to come up with a healthier way to think about the situation. Then write down your feelings again, and see if they have changed. (For examples of distressing thoughts and healthier alternatives, see the preceding two pages.)

Thought →	Feelings →	Healthier Thought →	Feelings
Date: Time 1: Time 2:			
Date: Time 1: Time 2:			
Date: Time 1: Time 2:			
Date: Time 1: Time 2:			

Date: Time 1: Time 2:			
Date: Time 1: Time 2:			
Date: Time 1: Time 2:			

Challenging Yourself to Face Your Fears

One of the most important techniques for overcoming your avoidance symptoms is to start facing the actual situations you are avoiding. This means you need to slowly start tackling your fears—both in terms of coping with upsetting situations and in terms of talking about the traumatic event(s) you've been through. You can start this process by identifying a large goal and breaking it down into smaller goals, using worksheet 20. You can review worksheet 14 and take a look at some of your larger goals. Choose one of these goals and break it down into smaller parts. Start by listing steps that make you the least anxious and build up to the steps that make you the most anxious. Rate each step from 0 to 10, with 0 being no anxiety at all and 10 being overwhelming, debilitating anxiety. Start with a step that you rate at 3 or less in order to build up your confidence. You should also plan ahead for what kinds of coping skills you'll use to get you through the challenges. To do this, review the skills presented in chapter 4 (for example, breathing, imagery) and decide which techniques will best help you cope with your anxiety as you slowly face your fears.

Worksheet 20: Facing Feared Situations

Purpose: To tackle your avoidance symptoms and start facing situations that frighten you.

Instructions: Choose an area of your life that is limited by PTSD and formulate a goal that will move your life beyond its current limits. You can use worksheet 14 to help guide you. Then think of four or five smaller steps that can bring you closer to that goal. You may want to use a separate sheet of paper to brainstorm the steps. Rate each of these steps on a scale of 0 (not anxiety-provoking) to 10 (would cause overwhelming anxiety), and list them on the worksheet in order from lowest rating to highest. Finally, write down which coping strategies you will use to help yourself navigate these steps toward your goal.

My Goal	Smaller Steps to Break It Down	How You Will Cope
Example 1: *Start dating again.*	1. *Start talking to guys I meet at the coffee shop, when it feels safe.* Anxiety=3/10 2. *Ask friends if they will set me up and double date with me.* Anxiety=5/10 3. *Go out alone with a male coworker or friend.* Anxiety=7/10 4. *Go on a date with a man I've never met before.* Anxiety=9/10	*I will remind myself that I can take my time before I trust someone.* *I will call Sally to tell her I got home safely.* *I will close my eyes and bring myself back to the moment if I feel myself getting panicky.*

Example 2: *Start driving again. I've been afraid since the car crash.*	1. *Sit in the car and start the engine.* Anxiety=*2*/10 2. *Drive to the grocery with my wife in the car.* Anxiety=*3*/10 3. *Drive to the grocery alone.* Anxiety=*5*/10 4. *Drive my children to the grocery store.* Anxiety=*7*/10 5. *Drive alone on the expressway.* Anxiety=*10*/10	*I will practice breathing to calm myself down.* *I will remind myself that I am facing my fears slowly, not all at once.*
	1. Anxiety = ____/10 2. Anxiety = ____/10 3. Anxiety = ____/10 4. Anxiety = ____/10 5. Anxiety = ____/10	
	1. Anxiety = ____/10 2. Anxiety = ____/10 3. Anxiety = ____/10 4. Anxiety = ____/10 5. Anxiety = ____/10	

Building Emotional Connections

Another symptom of PTSD is feeling emotionally numb. Sometimes it is difficult to connect with other people, particularly if you have been through something traumatic. You may feel that others don't understand you or that they are judging you. Perhaps you feel ashamed or guilty, unworthy of making friends and having relationships. This is another area where setting some specific goals can really help you live a healthier life.

In interactions with others, it is important to figure out what you want out of the encounter. For example, you might want to achieve a certain objective, you might want to preserve the relationship, or you might want to preserve your self-respect or values (Linehan 1993). Each interaction is different. When you want to achieve a certain objective, you can use assertive communication. That is, you can be very specific about what you want, but in a respectful way. If the relationship itself is the most important thing, then your approach would be very different. You would focus on listening to the other person and validating their feelings. Finally, if your self-respect is at stake, it is important not to compromise or apologize for your beliefs.

Worksheet 21: Connecting with Others

Purpose: To become more aware of how you interact with others.

Instructions: Describe your specific interactions with other people, including your goal for the interaction, any strategies you used, and reflections on how satisfied you were with how the encounter went. Do this once a day for at least two weeks (photocopy the worksheet so you have two weeks' worth of space; you can write on the back or use more paper if you need to).

Describe the Situation (Who Was Involved, What Was Said, How You Reacted)	What Was Your Goal?	What Strategies Did You Use?	Were You Satisfied with the Outcome? If Not, What Other Strategies Could You Have Used?
Example: *I went to the doctor's office to get a note for work, because I missed several days due to stress. My doctor doesn't know about my PTSD symptoms, and I didn't want to tell him. He seemed hesitant to give me the note, which really ticked me off. He finally wrote it, but it wasn't worded the way I wanted it.*	_X_ Meet my objective ____ Preserve the relationship ____ Preserve my self-respect *I wanted to get a doctor's note for my boss.*	*I didn't say much to my doctor. I just told him I had frequent headaches. I felt myself getting really angry and having trouble finding the right words.*	*I should have practiced what to say ahead of time. Maybe I could have told him I had something traumatic happen to me, I'm dealing with it, and I'm not comfortable saying more than that. I didn't think of it at the time.*

Date:	____ Meet my objective ____ Preserve the relationship ____ Preserve my self-respect		
Date:	____ Meet my objective ____ Preserve the relationship ____ Preserve my self-respect		
Date:	____ Meet my objective ____ Preserve the relationship ____ Preserve my self-respect		
Date:	____ Meet my objective ____ Preserve the relationship ____ Preserve my self-respect		
Date:	____ Meet my objective ____ Preserve the relationship ____ Preserve my self-respect		

Date:	____ Meet my objective ____ Preserve the relationship ____ Preserve my self-respect		
Date:	____ Meet my objective ____ Preserve the relationship ____ Preserve my self-respect		

Decreasing PTSD Symptoms through Writing

One of the most effective ways to deal with flashbacks and unwanted, painful thoughts related to trauma is to allow yourself to talk or write about the incident repeatedly. This technique works through the process of systematic desensitization. Your anxiety level will be high when you begin this journey. But as you go over the incident again and again, you will find you are able to cope with the painful thoughts and feelings. You will no longer have to live in fear of those memories; they will slowly lose their power over you. If you have lived through multiple traumatic events, it makes sense for you to choose the one that upsets you the most.

When you write about the trauma, be sure include as many details as you can. You can use your coping skills, including mindfulness, breathing, or using social support (for example calling a good friend) to help you deal with your feelings after each writing session. You should rate your anxiety level before and after each writing session. You can use what's called a *subjective unit distress scale* (SUDS), which asks you to rate your distress level from 0 to 10, where 0 is no distress at all and 10 is overwhelming distress. It is likely that your SUDS level will decrease after you write about the event over a period of weeks and months.

When your SUDS level comes down to a manageable level (say a 2 or 3), you will know the technique is working. It is important to remember that you will never get to the point where the memories are not difficult—the question is, are you able to cope the memories?

As you go through the process of writing, it is useful to identify your stuck points. Common stuck points are:

- Blaming yourself ("I should have known better"; "What was I thinking?")

- Difficulty processing what happened ("Bad things should not happen to good people")

- Beliefs about the future ("Horrible things will always happen to me"; "I cannot expect to ever have the things I want from life")

Once you identify your stuck points, you can see if you can challenge them with healthier, more balanced thoughts using the techniques we discussed in worksheet 19. Eventually, you can experiment with incorporating some of this new thinking into your writing.

Finally, it is important to plan ahead to use some healthy coping strategies each time you write about the traumatic event. You don't want to leave yourself overwhelmed and vulnerable to alcohol, drugs, or harming yourself. You can try the exercise in worksheet 22 on your own if you:

- Do not have a problem with drugs or alcohol.

- Have never had thoughts of suicide or harming yourself.

- Have a good social support system (friends and/or family you can talk with).

You should strongly consider doing these exercises with a trained mental health professional if:

- You use alcohol or drugs to cope with negative feelings.

- You have ever had thoughts of suicide.

- You have no friends or family to support you after you do the exercise.

Worksheet 22: Writing about Traumatic Experiences

Purpose: To stop avoiding trauma-related thoughts and memories and to learn how to cope constructively with painful flashbacks.

Instructions: In as much detail as possible, write about your traumatic event. Rate your distress level from 0 to 10 before and after the writing. Use additional paper if you need the space to write. You can make copies of this worksheet and complete the exercise once a day for a period of two weeks.

Your starting distress level: _____/10

What happened to you:

Your ending distress level: _____/10

A Final Note about Exposure Treatments

One interesting new development in exposure-based treatments is the use of virtual environments to simulate the sights and sounds of traumatic events. Again, this approach works using the principles of systematic desensitization. Some veterans' hospitals are using these techniques to help soldiers with PTSD. More information about this treatment is provided in the Resources section of this book.

Conclusion

Avoidance is a debilitating symptom of PTSD. Avoidance limits your life in so many ways, in terms of work, school, friends, and relationships. It keeps you from doing the things you truly value. The good news is that there are many techniques to help you tackle avoidance of your feelings, thoughts, and trauma-related memories. By incorporating some of these techniques into your life, you can truly take a huge step toward recovery. Chapter 6 will help you explore ways to manage upsetting memories, nightmares, and flashbacks. As you practice some of the exercises in chapters 4 through 6, you may find that you feel stuck and that you would like the help of a trained professional. Chapter 7 contains information about how to decide if you need professional help and how to find a therapist that is right for you.

Chapter 6

Coping with Painful Memories, Flashbacks, Nightmares, and Intrusions

One of the most frightening things about PTSD is that the symptoms can make you feel like you are experiencing the traumatic event all over again. Re-experiencing can take the form of upsetting memories, nightmares, and flashbacks (episodes when you feel the event is actually happening again). These reminders are emotionally and physically distressing. Most people with PTSD will do anything to avoid episodes of re-experiencing the trauma. In the last chapter, we discussed how to stop avoiding traumatic memories in order to start living life again. This chapter will focus on how to manage flashbacks and other types of re-experiencing without using avoidance. This may sound very challenging at first. But if you learn ways to successfully deal with re-experiencing, you won't have to live in fear of your symptoms. If something reminds you of the event, you will have techniques to take care of your emotional and physical reactions. This sense of mastery can be a huge relief. Most of these techniques use your mind as a tool to calm yourself down. You don't have to rely on just one of these techniques: try all of them and see which ones work for you. You can also combine these approaches into something that is tailored to your personality. After you have practiced these techniques, you will be able to plan ahead and to recognize your triggers. This doesn't mean avoiding people, places, or activities. It means being aware of situations that might affect you and practicing skills to take care of yourself in these challenging situations.

Focusing on Your Thoughts

A certain amount of re-experiencing is normal. Think of it this way: You have lived through something extremely difficult. It is completely normal for you to try to figure out why this happened and how to prevent it from happening again. The problem is that there are no easy answers to these questions. So in some ways, your brain is trying to process what has happened to you, but you are stuck in the event (in the form of nightmares, flashbacks, and painful memories) and can't get any answers. This is frustrating and frightening. However, one thing we know is that PTSD seems to be worse in people who try to avoid re-experiencing and in people who think it is not normal to think about the terrible events after they've happened (Malta et al. 2009).

When you experience painful memories, your thoughts, or the things you are saying to yourself about the episode, have a role to play. If you tell yourself things like "This is not normal" or "I absolutely need to stop thinking about this," it just tends to make you feel worse and to increase your symptoms. There is a classic psychology experiment in which the researchers told people to think about anything they wanted *except* a white bear. Can you guess what most people reported thinking about? Yes, most people were thinking about a white bear! Basically, by telling ourselves to avoid a topic, we make sure our brain wants to focus on it (Wegner et al. 1987). The lesson here is that pushing thoughts away doesn't work. Instead, a healthier approach is to simply notice trauma-related thoughts and pay attention to your reactions to having those thoughts.

Decatastrophizing

The next exercise will help you deal with your thoughts during flashbacks and painful memories. By reminding yourself that they are normal and won't last forever, you can actually help decrease their duration and intensity. This process is called *decatastrophizing*. *Catastrophizing* is a thought process in which you expect the worst in every situation. Decastastrophizing is the opposite process, in which you consider all the possibilities about a situation, particularly the neutral (and even the positive) ones.

Worksheet 23: Thoughts During Memories and Flashbacks

Purpose: To learn how you can use your thoughts to help you during painful memories and flashbacks.

Instructions: Next time you experience a flashback or painful memory, try to pay attention to what you are saying to yourself. See if you can use healthier, more compassionate ways of talking yourself through these situations. You can make copies of this worksheet and complete it once a day for two weeks or whenever you have painful memories or flashbacks.

Example:

Description of situation: *I saw my son playing by the sandbox. He looked so peaceful. Then, out of nowhere, I suddenly remembered being in the ambulance with him...how he couldn't breathe. I wanted to pick him up out of the sandbox and just run home with him.*

Specific thoughts: *This is totally abnormal. This happened months ago. I've got to put this out of my mind.*

Healthier thoughts: *Any mom would feel this way if she went through what I did. I know these memories won't last forever. Sure, it hurts to remember. But how could I forget? Forgetting what happened to him would be abnormal. My reaction is normal. My feelings are normal.*

Exercise:

1. Description of Situation:

Specific thoughts:

Healthier thoughts:

2. Description of Situation:

Specific thoughts:

Healthier thoughts:

3. Description of Situation:

Specific thoughts:

Healthier thoughts:

4. Description of Situation:

Specific thoughts:

Healthier thoughts:

5. Description of Situation:

Specific thoughts:

Healthier thoughts:

6. Description of Situation:

Specific thoughts:

Healthier thoughts:

7. Description of Situation:

Specific thoughts:

Healthier thoughts:

Invalidating Thoughts

The next exercise is similar to the last one, but has a different focus. Sometimes we can be our own worst critics. Invalidating thoughts are ways in which you might discourage and devalue yourself (Linehan 1993). Perhaps when you were young you had parents or caregivers who were not supportive of you. You may even be in this position as an adult. Invalidation takes many forms, including

- when you are told that you do not know what you are feeling or thinking (for example, when a child is repeatedly told she isn't hurt after being beaten)

- when you are told that your normal emotional and physical reactions are not acceptable or are weak (for example, when a child is told never to cry)

- when your needs are completely dismissed or ignored (for example, when a child is not fed or taken to school regularly)

- when you are severely criticized or severely punished for normal mistakes (for example, when a young child is repeatedly humiliated for spilling something or being messy).

Understandably, invalidation like this takes a toll. Eventually, the critical and hurtful voices of others can become a part of your own internal dialog (what you say to yourself) when you are older. When you have flashbacks or painful memories, you may be especially prone to these invalidating thoughts. For example, you may feel that you are not a good person or that you deserved something bad to happen to you. You might feel you are abnormal or that your trauma-related feelings and reactions are completely unjustified. Invalidating thoughts add to your emotional pain. Not only are you experiencing the pain of the traumatic memory, you are experiencing additional pain by blaming yourself, doubting yourself, or mistrusting your own judgments. The next exercise, worksheet 24, will help you to explore your invalidating thoughts and to generate alternate, more compassionate ways of thinking about yourself and what you've been though.

Worksheet 24: Changing Your Invalidating Thoughts

Purpose: To identify your invalidating thoughts and practice healthier, more compassionate ways of talking to yourself.

Instructions: Write down as many of your invalidating thoughts as you can over the course of several days. Try to examine them for a larger theme. Then, based on the theme, generate one or more alternative ways to think when you experience these thoughts. Write in a journal or carry a piece of paper with a note about which alternative thoughts you would like to remember, for easy reference.

Example:

Invalidating thoughts:

I can't do anything right.

Here I am being triggered again. I have no control.

I've got to get over this.

Why am I so weak? This happened a long time ago.

Themes:

It's not okay or normal to react. I don't deal with things properly.

Alternative Thoughts:

It is human to have emotions. I am a caring, feeling person. Showing my emotions actually takes courage!

Things to Remember:

Emotions take courage! I have courage for doing this.

Invalidating Thoughts:
- I'M NOT GOOD ξ MONEY
- I CAN'T HANDLE TOO MUCH
- CURRENT SOCIETY IS TOO MUCH FOR ME TO HANDLE
- I'VE DROPPED THE BALL – CAREER FINANCIAL SECURITY SO MANY MISSED OPPORTUNITIES
- SO MANY BAD DECISIONS IN LIFE

Themes:
- LIFE IS TOO OVERWHELMING, I CAN'T HANDLE A FULL, MODERN LIFE

Alternative Thoughts:
- LIFE CAN AT TIMES BE OVERWHELMING BUT I DIDN'T HAVE TOOLS & RESOURCES I NOW HAVE TO OVERCOME ANY CHALLENGE THAT COMES ALONG.
- AND I'VE EMERGED SUCCESSFUL DESPITE CHALLENGES!

Things to Remember (transfer to a journal or piece of paper you carry with you):
- I NOW HAVE TOOLS & RESOURCES I DIDN'T HAVE BEFORE
- I AM EQUIPPED TO HANDLE MODERN STRESSORS

Mindfulness and Grounding

Mindfulness techniques can help you cope during painful memories and can be used to ground yourself after flashbacks. Basically, this use of mindfulness builds on the skills introduced in chapter 4. Mindfulness is about paying attention to what is happening in each moment. So often, we spend time thinking about what has happened in the past and what will happen in the future: this is the opposite of mindfulness. Learning to bring yourself back to the moment is a great skill to help you cope with flashbacks and painful memories. And it is definitely a skill that needs to be tailored to your own personality and values. People find all sorts of objects, images, or senses can help ground them, or bring them back to the present moment. For example, John finds that looking at the American flag outside of his workplace reminds him that he is no longer in Iraq when he finds himself flashing back to the war. Erin finds that taking a deep breath and running her fingers over the smooth contour of the keys in her purse helps her to cope with overwhelming memories of a traumatic sexual assault. Mark reports that taking a drink of very cold water with a straw helps him focus back on the present moment and on his body when he has memories of a car accident he was in. The next exercise (worksheet 25) has some suggestions for how to use mindfulness and grounding to cope with painful memories and flashbacks. Try out the techniques suggested and see if you can add more to the list.

Worksheet 25: Mindfulness and Grounding Skills

Purpose: To use mindfulness and grounding skills to come back to the present moment during and after painful memories and flashbacks.

Instructions: The next time you have a painful flashback or memory, try one of the techniques listed below. Pay attention to as much detail as possible—what do you see, hear, taste, feel, and smell in the present moment? You can also create your own techniques to help you focus on the present moment, using objects or sounds around you. This worksheet has space to record your daily practice for a week; photocopy the page to practice longer. To rate your anxiety level, use a scale from 0 (no anxiety) to 10 (overwhelming anxiety).

Suggested Techniques:

1. Look out the window and observe what you see.

2. Look at your environment and try to describe the colors of the carpet, the walls, or whatever else is around you.

3. Listen to the sound of the clock on the wall.

4. Listen to your breath.

5. Listen to the sounds in your environment and try to describe what you hear.

6. Feel the soles of your feet on the floor. Pay attention to which parts of your foot are making contact with the floor.

7. Feel your body sitting in your chair—your legs touching the seat, your back making contact with the chair back.

8. Feel an object in your purse or pocket and describe the sensation in detail.

9. Feel the breeze on your arm. Notice the temperature and the sensation.

10. Rub your fingers over your face and hair and pay attention to the sensations.

11. Smell a calming scent or lotion that you carry with you.

12. Smell the air around you. Pay attention to the temperature.

13. Smell an orange, lemon, or apple. Pay attention to the aroma and describe it.

14. Sip a cold drink and pay attention to the feel of the liquid.

15. Put a mint or a piece of gum in your mouth and pay attention to the taste and sensations.

Grounding Practice Session 1

Level of anxiety before technique: _____/10

Technique used:

Level of anxiety after technique: _____/10

Notes on thoughts, feelings, and body sensations:

Grounding Practice Session 2

Level of anxiety before technique: _____/10

Technique used:

Level of anxiety after technique: _____/10

Notes on thoughts, feelings, and body sensations:

Grounding Practice Session 3

Level of anxiety before technique: _____/10

Technique used:

Level of anxiety after technique: _____/10

Notes on thoughts, feelings, and body sensations:

Grounding Practice Session 4

Level of anxiety before technique: _____/10

Technique used:

Level of anxiety after technique: _____/10

Notes on thoughts, feelings, and body sensations:

Grounding Practice Session 5

Level of anxiety before technique: _____/10

Technique used:

Level of anxiety after technique: _____/10

Notes on thoughts, feelings, and body sensations:

Grounding Practice Session 6

Level of anxiety before technique: _____/10

Technique used:

Level of anxiety after technique: _____/10

Notes on thoughts, feelings, and body sensations:

Grounding Practice Session 7:

Level of anxiety before technique: _____/10

Technique used:

Level of anxiety after technique: _____/10

Notes on thoughts, feelings, and body sensations:

Imagery Rehearsal

Nightmares are one of the most distressing features of PTSD. When you are not sleeping well, you are more likely to feel anxious, irritable, and depressed. Lack of sleep also takes a toll on your physical health and makes you more likely to experience short-term illnesses like colds and the flu, and also longer-term health problems (Pilcher and Ott 1998). If nightmares about your traumatic event(s) are keeping you awake, one approach you can try is called *imagery rehearsal*. This technique involves keeping track of your nightmares and practicing an alternate ending to them while you are awake. At some point, your brain will become used to thinking about the alternate ending, and it may help make your dreams less frightening (Krakow et al. 2000). The next exercise (worksheet 26) will help you understand how to use imagery rehearsal to ease your nightmares. If you are having difficulty finding an alternate ending, you may want to consult with a trained mental health professional to help you with this process.

Worksheet 26: Imagery Rehearsal for Nightmares

Purpose: To learn how to cope with painful and frightening nightmares.

Instructions: During the daytime (at a time when you are not sleeping or napping), in as much detail as you possible, write about your distressing dream. Rate your distress level from 0 to 10 before and after writing an alternate ending. Choose one of these options for practicing this ending (photocopy the worksheet so you can repeat your practice as often as necessary):

Option 1: Repeat writing about the nightmare (and alternate ending) every time you have it. You complete your writing in the daytime, at a time that you are not trying to sleep or nap. Rate your distress level before and after the alternate ending.

Option 2: Repeat writing about the nightmare every day. Underline places where you feel you are blaming yourself or places you feel stuck. Try to see if there are alternate ways to think about the situation. Practice incorporating these thoughts into the alternate ending.

Option 3: Use an audio recorder and read your alternate ending aloud. Listen to the recording every day for two weeks. Rate your distress level before and after each listening.

Example:

My dream: *I am at work in the Twin Towers. I'm at my desk. There is a yellow pad of paper on the desk. Suddenly I hear people talking louder and louder. It's chaotic. All of sudden I see James. I see Mr. Paudel. I can hear them screaming. I see people falling down the staircase. I see James crushed under some kind of hot cement. He's crying. His leg is bleeding. I feel helpless. I wake up sweating.*

My starting distress level: *9/10*

The alternate ending: *I hold on to James's hand and pull him out from the cement. We run down the stairs together. We run and can see the sunlight. We see our families. There is Margie, and Dawn. They hug us and kiss us. We feel their hands and faces. We are safe in their arms. We can feel them breathing.*

My ending distress level: *6/10*

Exercise:

My dream:

My starting distress level: _____/10

The alternate ending:

My ending distress level: _____/10

Developing Wise Mind

Now that you have some tools to help you cope with re-experiencing, you can also try to plan ahead for situations in which you might experience flashbacks or painful memories. Keep in mind that avoiding things you enjoy or need to do often makes you feel socially isolated, depressed, and more anxious in the long run. This technique is about how to anticipate what might upset you and plan ahead for healthy ways to cope. But how do you use your judgment to plan for these situations? Marsha Linehan (1993) has developed a very useful way to think about decision-making. Basically, we can all think about times when we have made a decision based purely on our emotions. In this case, you might be angry or upset and do something you really regret. Even positive emotions sometimes can lead you to unhappy outcomes. For example, you might feel love or overwhelming attraction for someone and do something you later regret. On the other hand, you can also think about decisions you make using only your rational thoughts. Perhaps you research which car is the most fuel efficient or what college is the most affordable. But in the end, the best decisions usually involve a combination of both your intellect and reason and your emotions and passion. For example, maybe you are really happy with the car you purchased. Not only is it fuel efficient, but is in a great red color and has the seat warmers you wanted! Perhaps you know the college you selected is a good value, but you can also envision yourself studying in those gorgeous ivy-covered buildings. Great decisions combine both reason and emotion, and combining and balancing the two is a skill that you need to develop and nurture. Some people call it a "gut instinct," and others call it "intuition." Still others feel it is the voice of God or divinity, or the universe.

Think about the last time you made a decision that helped you take care of yourself; a decision that was successful, compassionate, and reasonable. Try to apply this frame of mind to thinking about how to plan ahead for and cope with situations that might trigger your painful memories or flashbacks. For example, Steve has been very afraid of picking up friends from the airport since he experienced a serious plane crash two years ago. He is afraid that the sights and sounds of the airport will trigger him to have a panic attack. Emotionally, he feels irritated and angry when his wife asks him to pick up friends from the airport. Rationally, he know that his wife does not really understand how much he suffers from nightmares and flashbacks. If he trusts his gut instinct, Steve believes the next step is to talk to his wife. Maybe she can drive and he can be the passenger in the car when they pick up their friends at the airport. Based on his intuition, Steve knows that getting more social support is the first step in taking care of himself without avoiding life.

Worksheet 27: Planning Ahead

Purpose: To learn how to identify and plan ahead for emotionally upsetting situations and flashbacks.

Instructions: Think about the potential challenges you face in the coming week, and about how your emotion and reason would tell you to react to these challenges. Think about how you might combine your emotional and rational reactions to form a plan to cope. You can copy this worksheet and use it at the beginning of each week to plan for situations you may find emotionally difficult or challenging.

Example:

Anticipated challenge: *I am afraid that babysitting my nephew will remind me of what I went through when I was a kid. I am afraid I am going to cry and upset him.*

Emotional reaction: *Tell my sister I can't babysit.*

Rational reaction: *Realize I am a grown adult and should be able to take care of him for a few hours.*

Combined reaction: *Try spending a short time alone with him before babysitting for the whole afternoon. Put a picture of myself as an adult in my wallet so I can remind myself that I'm not a kid anymore. I can look at it if I feel myself getting overly emotional.*

Evaluation of the plan (after the situation): *This went pretty well. I did tear up a bit, but the picture was useful. Maybe my next plan should also involve talking to my sister about what I'm feeling to see if she has suggestions.*

Exercise:

1. Anticipated Challenge:

Emotional reaction:

Rational reaction:

Combined reaction:

Evaluation of plan (after the situation):

2. Anticipated Challenge:

Emotional reaction:

Rational reaction:

Combined reaction:

Evaluation of plan (after the situation):

3. Anticipated Challenge:

Emotional reaction:

Rational reaction:

Combined reaction:

Evaluation of plan (after the situation):

4. Anticipated Challenge:

Emotional reaction:

Rational reaction:

Combined reaction:

Evaluation of plan (after the situation):

Conclusion

Re-experiencing trauma you've been though is a very difficult symptom of PTSD. However, a certain amount of both emotional pain and re-experiencing is completely normal. You are a human being and are having human reactions to what you've lived through. Learning how to talk to yourself in a compassionate and kind manner can help you to deal with re-experiencing. Using grounding and mindfulness techniques can also help to shorten the duration and intensity of flashbacks. Similarly, practicing alternate endings to nightmares (during your waking hours) can help make them less frightening. Finally, learning to integrate your reason and your emotion will help you become skilled at taking care of yourself. If you can anticipate stressful situations and plan ahead for how you will handle them, you are one step closer to living the life you truly want.

Part 3

Surviving and Thriving as You Look Ahead

Chapter 7

How to Know Whether You Need Help from a Therapist

It can be very difficult to decide whether you need professional help to recover from your trauma. You might feel that you should be able to handle things on your own or that talking to someone means you are not a strong person. You might also be worried that talking about your trauma in treatment will actually make your symptoms worse. There are a few key things to remember. A good therapist will let you set the pace of treatment, and will not force you discuss things you are not ready for. Also, evidence-based treatments are built on your developing good coping skills before you delve into trauma-related memories. Finally, take a good look at the way you think about emotional strength. Sure, it's important to try to tackle your own problems. The sense that you can manage your feelings and emotions well (a sense of *self-efficacy*) is a key part of healing. But it's also important to know when you need to reach out for some help. Emotional strength is about leaning to cope on your own, and also about learning how (and when) to lean on others. Therapy can be a good opportunity to learn both aspects of emotional strength—independence and reliance on those you trust.

Do You Need Professional Help?

One of the best ways to determine if you should seek therapy is to consider how much your symptoms are interfering with your daily life. For example, are you having trouble at school or work? Are you having difficulty forming close relationships with people? If you feel overwhelmed with sadness or if you've ever had thoughts about hurting yourself or ending your life, you should seek therapy. If you are dealing with feelings of rage and have thought about seriously hurting another person, you should also seek therapy. A trained professional can help you to find ways to deal with those feelings. You should also get help if you are using alcohol or drugs (prescription or street drugs) to cope with your symptoms. Although substance use helps in the short term to numb you to feelings of sadness or anxiety, in the long term it simply makes it more difficult to function from day to day. For example, although drinking several drinks every evening may help you cope with anxiety and help you to fall asleep, this same behavior almost always has a downside. You might find that you wake up very easily in the middle of the night, and that the anxiety you suffer when you are sober is even worse.

If you experience periods of serious *dissociation*, you should also seek professional help. Dissociation can include feeling strongly detached from your body, emotionally numbness, or having significant difficulty remembering things. Perhaps you suffer from flashbacks or painful memories that are so intense that you lose long periods of time. On a related note, you may have extreme difficulty concentrating or sleeping, and this might be affecting your ability to work, go to school, or have relationships. A trained professional can help you work on these types of symptoms. They are difficult to tackle on your own.

In general, a good way to figure out if you need therapy is to take a look at how you are functioning on a day-to-day basis. For example, are you able to go to work and school every day? When you are there, are you able to focus and concentrate? Do you have close relationships? Do you struggle to get close to people and deal with significant periods of irritability, sadness, or anger? If you feel like your work and personal life is being significantly impacted by the aftermath of trauma, you should seriously consider talking to a mental health professional. You can use the worksheet that follows (worksheet 28) to help you decide if you need more help. The worksheet can also help you start a conversation with a therapist about which symptoms bother you the most and where to focus your discussion.

Worksheet 28: Should I Seek Therapy?

Purpose: To ask yourself some key questions to help you decide if you need mental health treatment.

Instructions: Consider the questions below. If you answer yes to any of them, you should strongly consider contacting a professional for more help in working on your symptoms and developing the life you want.

Do you use substances including alcohol or drugs (prescription or street drugs) to help you cope? Yes No

Do you have serious thoughts about hurting yourself? Yes No

Do you have self-harming thoughts on a regular basis? Yes No

Do you have a specific plan about how you will act on self-harming thoughts? Yes No

Do you have serious thoughts about hurting someone else? Yes No

Do you have thoughts of hurting someone else on a regular basis? Yes No

Do you have a specific plan about how you will act on thoughts of hurting someone else? Yes No

Do you have significant periods when you feel out of touch with your body or your thoughts? Yes No

Do you have considerable difficulty experiencing any feelings or emotions? Yes No

Do you have significant trouble concentrating when you need to? Yes No

Do you feel that you are unable to function in an important domain of your life—for example, at work, school, or home, or in your relationships with people? Yes No

Finding the Right Therapist

Perhaps you have decided that seeking therapy is your next step. Remember that not all therapists have training in dealing with PTSD and trauma. Therapists have varying levels of training as well as varying backgrounds.

- Psychiatrists have a medical degree (MD). They can prescribe medications and are sometimes trained in psychotherapy. Not all are trained specifically in PTSD or trauma.

- Licensed clinical psychologists have a PhD or PsyD degree. In most states they cannot prescribe medication. Most are trained in psychotherapy, but not all are trained specifically in how to treat trauma or PTSD.

- Licensed clinical social workers (LCSWs) can have bachelors (BA/BS), masters (MA/MS) or doctoral (DSW, PhD) degrees. Some are trained in psychotherapy and others focus on case management. Not all are trained specifically in how to treat trauma or PTSD.

- Some states license providers who have a bachelors or associates degree. Most of these providers are not specifically trained in treating PTSD or trauma.

Here are some tips to use when trying to find a therapist who is trained and experienced in treating PTSD and other effects of trauma.

- Ask supportive friends, family members, or coworkers for a referral.

- Take a look at reputable websites (a few are suggested in the Resources section of this book) for a list of trained providers.

- Online Listservs and social networking communities that are focused on PTSD and trauma can provide you with referrals.

- If you have health insurance that covers mental health treatments, ask your carrier for a list of covered mental health care providers in your area. Providers may have areas of expertise listed in their profiles, which can help you narrow down the list.

Once you find a few providers, make contact. Pay attention to how the person makes you feel when you are talking with him or her on the phone. It is important that you feel your provider is empathic, kind, and a good listener. In addition, it helps to know what sort of experience he or she has in treating survivors of trauma. In worksheet 29 is a list of some questions you can use to interview possible therapists, either on the phone or at an initial appointment.

Remember that a good therapist will welcome these types of questions. A client who asks questions is an informed one! There isn't a right or wrong answer to these questions— choosing a therapist comes down to the fit between a client's needs and preferences and a therapist's background and style. For example, some clients prefer a younger therapist who has recently trained at a nationally recognized medical center. Some clients might feel more comfortable with a clinician who has had years of experience treating trauma. You may feel that you do not want someone who prescribes medications, or you may feel that this might be an important step in your healing. The point of the interview guide is to help you talk to potential providers about how they view therapy and how they view change. It is a step toward finding someone who has the right listening skills, level of experience, and background to work well with you.

Worksheet 29: Provider Interview Guide

Purpose: To find a therapist who is right for you.

Instructions: Ask the following questions when you talk to a potential therapist on the telephone or at the first appointment. Add your own questions as well; for example, "Have you worked with combat veterans?" Take notes on each therapist's answers. Photocopy this sheet to use it more than once.

How often do you treat PTSD and trauma?

What approach do you use in therapy?

Do you prescribe medications?

How many years have you been in practice?

What is your degree in? Are you licensed or board certified? Where did you train?

Do you use CBT/DBT/ACT techniques?

Other questions

Other notes

Conclusion

Making the decision to seek mental health treatment is not necessarily easy. The intensity of your symptoms and your level of daily impairment are good guides in helping you decide if you should work with a professional. Not all mental health practitioners have experience treating trauma, and not all have specific experience using CBT, DBT, or ACT techniques. It is important to ask questions of potential providers to find someone who makes you feel comfortable and helps you improve the quality of your life.

Chapter 8

How to Take Better Care
of Your Health

When you have experienced a traumatic event, it can take a toll on your physical health as well as your mental health. In fact, there is strong evidence that people with PTSD tend to deal with a lot of health problems. You might also find that you don't seem to pay much attention to your lifestyle choices and your health. This is understandable. One symptom of PTSD is a sense of *foreshortened future*. What that means is that you might not expect to live as long as other people—you may feel that your future is going to be cut short. You might also not expect to achieve the same milestones as other people—whether that means getting married, having children, having a successful career, or having a stable retirement. Trauma can limit your ability to think about the future and your capacity for hope. It is not uncommon to meet veterans who feel that they will not live past the age of fifty, even when they've made it out of a war zone alive. A survivor of sexual assault might feel that she doesn't deserve good things to happen to her, or that she will never graduate from school or form meaningful relationships.

Improving Your Overall Health and Quality of Life

Once you begin to tackle your symptoms using the approaches suggested in this book, you can also begin to work on improving the overall quality of your life and physical health. This means moving beyond a simple focus on symptom management. It means focusing on prevention and good self-care. Once you get some relief from your symptoms of PTSD, you should consider what you are doing to take care of your body and spirit. Taking care of your body also will improve your mood and your ability to cope with stressful situations. Taking care of your physical health is another way to improve your emotional health, because the mind and the body are connected.

Remember that change does not have to be an "all or nothing" proposition. It is more important to make small changes that you can continue long term than make big changes that last for only a few days. For example, it's not necessary to give up all junk food or stop smoking cigarettes cold turkey. It makes more sense to cut back gradually. People are much more likely to experience success when they approach change in this way (Miller and Rollnick 2002). In addition, you should feel free to tailor the suggestions presented here to your own lifestyle and personality. They are intended only to get you thinking about the topic of health. Only you know what specific techniques will work in your own life.

Nutrition and Exercise

One aspect of self-care is good nutrition. If you are using food as a way to cope with traumatic memories, consider whether there are healthier ways that you can cope. Perhaps you can unwind by watching your favorite television show, or you can go for a short walk. If you are reluctant to give up food as a way of coping, see if you can make your snacks or meals a bit more healthy. For example, alternate a glass of water after each glass of soda. Or eat potato chips on some days and popcorn on other days. You don't need to make huge changes to start taking better care of yourself. The Resources section of this book lists some websites that can guide you toward healthy eating patterns.

Like good nutrition, regular exercise is a basic aspect of self-care and good health. As outlined in chapter 4, there are some basic steps you can take to increase your activity level, even in small doses. Think about ways that you can increase your activity without retriggering your PTSD symptoms. For example, parking your car farther away from a store entrance and walking may seem like a good idea at first. However, perhaps your feelings of anxiety will be very high if you are walking alone in a parking lot. Upon reflection, you may find other ways to build activity into your life. For example, maybe you watch television every evening. If you decide to stretch and jog in place during the commercials, you will be increasing your activity level in small, manageable, and non-anxiety-provoking way. Here is a list of suggestions for increasing your daily activity level. Evaluate these ideas based on your individual situation and symptoms and find what works for you:

- Use the stairs instead of the elevator.

- Walk around the block once a day.

- Stretch or do some light exercise while watching television.

- Take a walk with a coworker several times a week.

- Dance or play tag with your kids.

- Stand up when you are talking on the phone.

- Garden, or do yard work or housework.

- Wash your car.

Sleep

Developing good sleeping habits can help you deal with nightmares and improve the overall quality of your health (Lavie 2001).

- If possible, go to bed at the same time and get up at the same time every day. This may take many weeks to get used to, but it can help you develop a sleep routine.

- If possible, sleep in a room that is free from distractions, including the television and other electronic devices.

- If possible, sleep in a room that is fairly dark (as dark as is comfortable for you) and is a relatively cool and comfortable temperature.

- If you are awake for more than thirty minutes in the middle of the night, get up and do something else in another room. This will stop you from worrying about not sleeping (which doesn't help you sleep) and provide you with a distraction.

- If you have a period of insomnia, do not sleep later to "make up" for your lost sleep. This disrupts your overall sleep pattern and does not let your body adjust to a routine.

Medical Care and Prevention

Another part of becoming healthier is going to your doctor regularly. This can be really challenging when you have PTSD symptoms. Traumatic events almost always involve something happening to your body, and they leave you feeling that you or someone else is going to be seriously harmed. So when you go to the doctor, it's normal to feel triggered, or reminded of your trauma. Because of this, many survivors put off going to the doctor and don't engage in the preventative care that they need to. Sometimes survivors don't get regular mammograms, cervical or colon cancer screenings (Pap smears, colonoscopies), or dental check-ups. You might feel anxious before going to the appointment, worry about how you will react physically during an invasive procedure, or worry about feeling powerless.

So how can you approach becoming more comfortable with going to the doctor or dentist? The first step is to find someone you feel comfortable with. The process is similar to finding a therapist: focus on finding someone with the right mix of technical knowledge and interpersonal skills. Here are some tips:

- A good doctor will welcome your questions.

- A good doctor will answer your questions using plain, understandable language.

- A good doctor will make you feel comfortable and will be understanding of your anxiety or other reactions.

Not every trauma survivor worries about doctor and dental appointments, but some do. Once you find a doctor you are comfortable with, it is up to you to decide how much of your trauma history you want to share. You don't have to tell the doctor you are a survivor of something traumatic unless you feel comfortable doing so. If you decide to tell you doctor, practice ahead of time how much detail you are willing to reveal about the experience. You might even find it useful to write out what you are going to say (and not say) ahead of time. If you decide not to tell your doctor what you've been through, you can simply say that certain procedures make you nervous. Here are some ways you can make your medical and dental appointments more comfortable:

- Ask your doctor to explain how the appointment will flow and what to expect during a specific procedure.

- Ask the doctor if you can come up with a signal to indicate that you are in any discomfort, and whether he or she can stop a procedure (or give you a short break), if necessary.

- Think about how you can cope with anxiety. Consider calling upon the exercises in chapter 4 before and during the appointment. You can plan to use techniques like deep breathing, distraction, or simply observing the thoughts you are having.

Finding Meaning, Purpose, and Social Support

Finally, when it comes to taking care of our health, there is a lot we can learn from resilient people. In the area of PTSD, *resiliency*—the ability to heal and grow after stress —is called *post-traumatic growth*, or *adversarial growth* (Linley and Joseph 2004), and it's received a lot of attention in recent years. Obviously, no one would ever voluntarily choose to live through something traumatic. However, once it happens, resilient people tend to think about how their traumatic experiences will fit into a bigger picture in their lives, and how their lives can have a sense of meaning and purpose. That purpose might be related to what they've lived through, or it might be about something else entirely. People who focus on getting involved in their communities, supporting a cause they believe in, or working for social change can experience a lot of benefits, in terms of both their physical and mental health. For example, after getting her symptoms under control, a sexual abuse survivor might decide to volunteer at an organization for at-risk kids. A veteran might decide to get involved in a local group to lobby Congress for more funding for PTSD and veterans' programs. A survivor of gun violence may decide that her true calling is to spend more time at home, and volunteering at her daughter's school. The key is finding something that fits for you—something that is deeply meaningful, but not overwhelming emotionally and spiritually. For example, Megan, a sexual assault survivor, feels that volunteering at a rape crisis center is too triggering and emotionally upsetting. Instead, she decides to volunteer at a senior center, spending time playing cards with and serving meals to residents. She always had a close relationship with her grandmother, so spending time with seniors is a way for Megan to feel useful and needed. Megan also joins a Listserv for assault survivors and writes letters to her congressman urging stronger penalties for perpetrators of violence. Megan has found a way to get involved and find purpose in a way that is emotionally healing and not overwhelming.

Feeling connected to others is also an important aspect of resilience. Resilient people are not afraid to get the social support they need. This means seeking support from community, friends, and/or family. Of course, when you have PTSD, connecting to other people can be really difficult. Some people take the first step by joining a support group for people with PTSD—for example, a group for veterans or a group for survivors of crime. The Resources section of this book has some suggestions on issue-specific social support.

Of course, support doesn't always have to be focused on PTSD. Many people with PTSD benefit from generally increasing their level of social activity. For example, you can join a club or other organization that is based on something you are interested in. This can feel overwhelming, but often the biggest challenge is simply getting started. Once you start attending an activity, you may find that eventually you look forward to it. The key is not to wait until you feel like you want to attend. As strange as it may seem, sometimes you have to change your behavior first, and wait for your feelings to catch up later. Remember that you do not have to talk about your PTSD or trauma history in various social gatherings. It can be useful to think in advance about what details of your life you are comfortable talking about, and what you would rather not discuss until you know someone well. Thinking about this ahead of time can help you feel a little more at ease in new social situations. Chapter 9 has a longer discussion on social support.

Worksheet 30: Self-Care for Healthy Coping

Purpose: To think about ways to improve your overall health.

Instructions: Place a check mark in front of the suggestions you would like to try, and add other options to the lists below.

Diet and Exercise Suggestions

☐ Increase water intake.

☐ Increase fruit/vegetable intake.

☐ Take vitamins daily.

☐ Decrease junk food (specify what food and/or at what times of day):

☐ Increase daily activity (specify how; for example, "Stand up while I'm talking on the phone").

☐ Increase exercise level (specify what you will do, how often, and how long).

☐ Other nutrition and exercise related ideas:

Suggestions for Health Care and Doctors Visits

☐ Tell my doctor about my PTSD symptoms.

☐ Tell my doctor about my traumatic event(s).

☐ Ask my doctor to explain all the parts of the appointment.

☐ Ask my doctor for start/stop signals to use if I get anxious.

☐ Make an appointment for preventative care (specify when and what type):

☐ Other health care ideas:

Suggestions for Finding Meaning

☐ Volunteer (specify where and how often):

☐ Lobby for a political change (specify how; for example, "letter writing to my congressman"):

☐ Join an organization or Listserv (specify which):

☐ Become more active in a spiritual tradition (specify what tradition, and what you would do):

☐ Other ideas for finding meaning:

Suggestions for Getting Social Support

☐ Join a club or organization based on your interests (specify which organization/which kind of organization):

☐ Join a PTSD support group (specify which group/which kind of group):

☐ Other social support ideas:

Conclusion

Part of healing from PTSD is taking better care of your body and spirit. Once your symptoms are under control, it is important to think about prevention in addition to symptom management. This means eating well, exercising, and going to your doctor regularly. It means thinking about a deeper meaning and purpose for your life, which can include volunteering and social activism. It also means getting social support, which can be focused on PTSD or focused simply on companionship and common interests. Trauma doesn't have to define who you are, but it is something profound that you have lived through. Finding ways to survive and thrive is challenging, but it is very possible.

Chapter 9

How to Get More Support

No one can heal all alone. This may seem like an obvious thing to say, but it's particularly important to remember and to think about in relation to living with PTSD. When you have experienced a traumatic event, your assumptions about how the world works are challenged on a very basic level. Often, a lot of your challenges have to do with how much you can trust other people and how much other people can relate to your emotional pain. Developing a good social support system is hard for many people. We live in a culture that values individualism and stresses independence. Although these are important values, it is equally important to have at least a few people in your life who you value and trust.

The first step in figuring out if you need to develop more social support is to examine the level of support you have now. The following worksheet (worksheet 31) can help you explore this issue.

Worksheet 31: Types of Support

Purpose: To identify areas where you have good social support, and areas where you may want to expand your support network.

Instructions: Based on your experiences, answer the questions below. Use the answers to help you think about whether you would like to increase your support in various areas.

Do you have friends whom you socialize with regularly (at least once a month)?

None   Very few (1 or 2)   Some (3 to 5)   A lot (more than 5)

How satisfied are you with this area of support? (Circle one)

Not at all satisfied   Somewhat satisfied   Very satisfied

Do you have family members who you socialize or interact with regularly (at least once a month)?

None   Very few (1 or 2)   Some (3 to 5)   A lot (more than 5)

How satisfied are you with this area of support? (Circle one)

Not at all satisfied   Somewhat satisfied   Very satisfied

Do you attend activities at least once a month (for example, church, clubs, other hobbies in a social setting) where you interact with other people?

None   Very few (1 or 2)   Some (3 to 5)   A lot (more than 5)

How satisfied are you with this area of support? (Circle one)

Not at all satisfied   Somewhat satisfied   Very satisfied

Do you have people you can rely on when you need things (for example, for money, shelter, help around the house, babysitting)?

None   Very few (1 or 2)   Some (3 to 5)   A lot (more than 5)

How satisfied are you with this area of support? (Circle one)

Not at all satisfied   Somewhat satisfied   Very satisfied

Do you have people you can rely on emotionally (for example, to listen to you when you have a problem, to give you advice when you want it, to tell you they care about you)?

None   Very few (1 or 2)   Some (3 to 5)   A lot (more than 5)

How satisfied are you with this area of support? (Circle one)

Not at all satisfied   Somewhat satisfied   Very satisfied

The next step is to use the information you gathered from worksheet 31 to think about where you would like to expand your social support network. Basically, if you have a few friends you socialize with and you feel very satisfied with that arrangement, then you do not need to think about changing this area. However, if you feel you do not have anyone to provide you with emotional support and you are not satisfied with that, you may want to think about some of the techniques we are going to discuss.

It is helpful to think about social support on a continuum (see figure 5). On one end, you have acquaintances, who are people we see from time to them. They may share a few of your interests, but in general, they don't know you (and you don't know them) very well. On the other end are people whom you feel very close to. These are people you can rely on if you need help or emotional support. They are also people you enjoy being around (for the most part) and people who share some of your interests and values. All points of the social support continuum are valuable, and a strong social support system often contains acquaintances and casual friends as well as closer relationships.

There are three key points to remember about getting social support. First of all, you don't need the same person or people to meet all of your needs. For example, it's great if you have a friend who will give you a ride when you need one and another person who will listen to you if you have a bad day. The same person doesn't need to fulfill all those functions—in fact, it sometimes works best for everyone if one person is not the go-to for another person's every need. The second point is that though you may have many acquaintances, it's fine to have far fewer close friends. In fact, most people don't have more than a handful of people on the bottom end of the continuum, and that is perfectly healthy. The third point is that it is very common for people with PTSD to have difficulty with many types of relationships. You may find it difficult to connect with acquaintances, feeling that the relationship has no real depth or meaning (based on what you've lived through), and you may find that you don't have a lot of close relationships (due to issues with trust, anger, irritability, anxiety, or depression). Don't be too hard on yourself. Use the exercises from chapters 4 and 5 to take a look at some of your thoughts and feelings. When you are ready to start working on these issues, you can begin to make some changes to strengthen and deepen your social support system.

Acquaintances:

people you see on a passing basis; you know fairly little about them and are generally limited to one or two general topics of conversation or "small talk"

Closer relationships:

people with whom you have a one-on-one relationship; you share interests and values, but you do not rely on each other for emotional or other types of support; you might talk about general life stressors, but not specifically your trauma history

Casual friends:

people you see from time to time in social or work settings; you rarely have one-on-one contact with each other; you talk about your life on a general level

Close relationships:

people with whom you have a one-on-one relationship; you have shared interests and values and you rely on each other for emotional or other types of support; you can discuss your trauma history or other life stressors

Figure 5: The Continuum of Support

When you look at this continuum, you may find that you are lacking one or more types of relationships. When you have PTSD, it's important to consider how much of your personal life you are willing to share. There is no easy answer to this question. For example, if you are a veteran with a history of trauma in combat, perhaps you have chosen not to tell your acquaintances that you served in the military. Or perhaps you decided to stick to some very brief, nonrevealing information about yourself. In casual settings, trauma does not have to define you. For example, a veteran might say, "Yes, I served in Afghanistan, but I don't talk about it much. Tell me about you." The key thing to consider is what and how much about yourself you want to share. It's better if you think about this ahead of time, rather than when you are actually in a social situation. It can very tough to be in a social setting without a rehearsed answer about something that has to do with your PTSD or trauma. Keep in mind that "rehearsed" doesn't have to be a negative or false thing. It just means being somewhat emotionally prepared for how much of your experiences you are willing to discuss with the people in your life. Of course, how much you discuss should depend on how close the relationship is. Basically, a traumatic event is something that is personal—you do not need to discuss it in a casual setting. This doesn't mean you need to be ashamed of it, or that not talking about it in all settings means you are hiding it. It means you need to honor what you've been through enough to understand that you get to choose who you discuss it with.

Something else to be aware of is that if you want to move a relationship toward the "close" end of the continuum, there needs to be mutual sharing and trust. You can start the process of building trust slowly. Start by sharing something about yourself that does not have to do with your trauma. For example, a woman who is dealing with the loss of her child in a sudden accident might choose to talk to an acquaintance about her job stress. If her acquaintance reacts with empathy and caring, it's a sign that the relationship may become closer. However, if the acquaintance seems overwhelmed and disinterested, it is a good sign that the relationship will remain in the current state. The key is to start out with less emotionally charged issues and see how the other person responds to you.

On a related note, once you start to look at the quality of your relationships, you may begin to see that some relationships are not healthy for you. For example, if a person is actively unsupportive, puts you down, or abuses you physically or emotionally, you should end that relationship. Some signs a relationship is unhealthy include:

- Feeling like you are always giving support, but do not receive any.

- Feeling emotionally drained after almost all of your encounters with the other person.

- Feeling that the other person constantly belittles you, puts you down, or makes you feel inferior.

- Being threatened by the other person with physical, emotional, or financial harm.

If this is happening to you, consider talking with a therapist to discuss ways to get more positive support in your life. It is very difficult to be able to heal from trauma when you have someone who is retraumatizing you in your life.

Finally, if you want to move toward closer relationships, it's also important to remember to offer support as well as receive it. Think about your own strengths and weaknesses and remember that a good friend doesn't need to fulfill every need. Perhaps you are someone who is very organized. For you, being a good friend could mean sending a card to a friend who is having a tough time, or being the one to remember family birthdays. Perhaps you are a great listener. In that case, you can be someone who can offer a sympathetic ear (in amounts of time that do not feel emotionally overwhelming) to a friend in need. Or perhaps you are good at fixing things, and don't mind helping out friends from time to time when they need a hand. The basic point is that if you want to have relationships on the "close" end of the continuum, you and the other person both need to do things to invest in the relationship.

Trusting others is not easy, particularly for people with PTSD. But trust and connection are essential parts of being alive and healing. Remember that you have the ability to decide how much of yourself you want to share in a relationship. If you are interested in creating closer relationships, consider seeing how the person reacts to less threatening information and decide if you think they will be supportive. Finally, remember that you can also be a friend and offer support. Indeed, helping other people can be an important part of healing.

If Someone You Love Has PTSD: Advice for Family and Friends

The final section of this chapter is for friends and family members who want to support a loved one with PTSD. Helping someone deal with the aftermath of trauma can be overwhelming on many levels. It is normal for you to have times when you feel angry, upset, frightened, and emotionally overwhelmed. This section has several suggestions for helping your loved one who has PTSD. First, though, there are a few important things to remember for yourself.

People with PTSD symptoms may experience intense periods of anger, and this can be extremely frightening—especially if you witness those periods of anger and rage, or you are a target of the anger. If you feel that your loved one is putting you or other people in danger, you need to seek help. Although you may really want to help them, it is not healthy for you to put yourself in harm's way. You should not sacrifice your own physical safety to help someone with PTSD. It is important for you to seek help from a specialist trained in PTSD to form a plan to protect your safety. The Resources section of this book contains information on where you can find help.

You need to take good care of yourself if you are going to help someone else, particularly someone who is dealing with an intense emotional issue like trauma. When you get on an airplane, you are advised that you need to put on your own oxygen mask before helping anyone else to put their mask on, even your children. This is a good metaphor for caregivers to remember. You can't be helpful to someone else if you are overly tired and stressed. It's important to focus on good nutrition, exercise, and your own social support as you help your loved one. Some people find issue-specific support helpful. For example, some spouses of veterans have formed support groups. Other people prefer to stay involved in their existing community and participate in other types of social activities. It doesn't matter where you get your support, it just matters that you do. In fact, having a good mix of acquaintances and close friends (see figure 5) can definitely help.

Finally, if you yourself are a survivor of traumatic events, it's important that you seek help for your own trauma. Again, you cannot be supportive of someone else's journey if you are being triggered and experiencing your own difficult-to-manage symptoms. You may not realize when your own issues are being brought up, so it's important to start thinking about this issue.

It can be truly challenging to help someone with PTSD. You want to find the right balance between listening, encouragement, and acceptance of their feelings. It's important for family and friends to take a close look at their own attitudes about trauma. For example, maybe you wish your loved one could move on and "get over it." It is normal for family and friends to have thoughts like these. However, you need to be careful about what you say along these lines and how you say it. There is evidence that hearing these kinds of sentiments expressed can actually make survivors experience higher levels of depression, anxiety, and PTSD symptoms (Ullman and Filipas 2001). Survivors are often dealing with guilt and self-blame already. In addition, they are often hard on themselves about the time it takes to heal. It's not uncommon for people with PTSD to feel "crazy," expressing sentiments like "I should just be able to get over this." It's more useful to let them know that any normal person would have a reaction to what they have been through, and that healing takes time. Here are some suggestions for supportive responses you can use with a loved one who has PTSD:

- "I'm sorry you went through that."

- "Let me know what I can do. Or if I can just listen."

- "What happened was not your fault."

- "Anyone would have reactions to the things you've been through. It is understandable that this isn't easy for you."

- "I do not know all the answers, but I am here for you."

Survivors have reported that reactions that are stigmatizing and distracting tend to make them feel worse about themselves. For example, although a loved one might say "Get on with your life" or "You need to stop talking about this" in a well-intentioned way, a survivor might experience the remark very negatively. Be careful of messages that might make the survivor feel like you are blaming them or that you don't want them to talk about what they've been through. Remember, if they could move on easily, they certainly would. Recovery takes time, patience, and plenty of social support.

If you want to be supportive of someone with PTSD, here are some general tips:

- Correct misinformation and victim-blaming attitudes when you encounter them. You can be a great source of education to other people. It's important to try to correct people when you hear them downplay the seriousness or the effects of trauma. Standing up for your loved one is a great way to show support and start changing people's attitudes.

- Encourage your loved one to become more healthy, but don't push them. If they are making small changes, praise those. Try not to point out all of their shortcomings. They are likely already aware of all the things they are not doing to take care of themselves. Consider joining your loved one in a small behavioral change—for example, daily exercise, meditation, or prayer. This is a great way to show support.

- Listen to your loved one, but remember you are not their therapist. If you feel overwhelmed and burnt out, gently suggest that your loved one seek treatment. It is perfectly okay to set limits around how much you can hear and how much advice you can give.

- Don't jump in with your own trauma story when your loved one is talking in depth about what happened. It's human nature to want to let a survivor know you understand them—and to perhaps give details of a traumatic event you've experienced or heard about. Resist this urge: a survivor doesn't need to deal with another traumatic event while their own memories are still fresh.

- Do not press your loved one for details of the traumatic event(s). Remember that good coping skills are needed before a person can handle all the difficult feelings that come up when talking about trauma. If your loved one feels strong enough to talk about the trauma, then by all means listen. You do not need to find out exactly what happened in order to be supportive of their current functioning and healing.

- Protect your own mental health. Remember that you cannot do any good for another person without taking care of yourself. This means getting rest and exercise, eating right, and dealing with your own emotional issues.

- Protect your own safety. Never put yourself in harm's way, even if your loved one's PTSD symptoms play a role. Seek professional help about ways to stay safe.

- Finally, be yourself. If you don't know what to say, just admit that. Give the survivor a chance to talk. Even therapists specializing in PTSD do not have all the answers about why certain things happen, and you do not need to have those answers either. Sometimes having the comfort of another person nearby who cares is enough.

Conclusion

Although PTSD is about anxiety and fear, it is also about a lack of connection. Finding ways to develop friendships as well as acquaintances is a part of healing. Remember that your trauma history is one aspect of your life, and you do not need to share it with everyone. You can choose the people and settings in which you talk about trauma. It's important to give emotional support as well as let others know how they can support you. Family and friends need to engage in good self-care, encouragement, and listening to help loved ones with PTSD. The bottom line is that connection to others is an essential part of healing from trauma.

Afterword

The purpose of this book is to present you with the latest techniques to help you deal with trauma and PTSD. Chapters 1 and 2 give you an overview of PTSD and trauma, including the prevalence and nature of trauma-related symptoms. Chapters 3 through 6 encourage and equip you to experiment with cognitive behavioral therapy (CBT), dialectical behavior therapy (DBT), and acceptance and commitment therapy (ACT) techniques to find an approach that works for you. It's important to find something that is tailored to your needs, because no one has lived through your exact set of circumstances, and no one has your exact personality. At the same time, you are not alone. Many people have experienced traumatic events, and many people have survived and thrived—using skills and support in a way that works for them. Hopefully, this book has helped you practice a wide variety of approaches to your symptoms. Some exercises here focus on your behavior and others focus on your thoughts. Some exercises encourage you to change your thoughts, while others encourage you to observe and accept difficult thoughts and emotions. With time and commitment, you can find a set of techniques that works best for you. Chapters 7, 8, and 9 remind you that symptom management is not the end of the road. When it comes to recovery and healing, you also need to focus on getting social support, often including professional therapeutic support and help, and on improving your overall health.

Traumatic events are horrible, painful experiences. But human beings have an amazing capacity for growth and resilience. We have an incredible ability to educate others, to form deep bonds with those around us, and to find meaning in our lives. I hope this book has given you some techniques to explore this potential and live the life you truly want.

Resources

General Information

The National Center for Posttraumatic Stress Disorder: www.ptsd.va.gov

Dialectical Behavior Therapy: behavioraltech.org/resources/whatisdbt.cfm

Acceptance and Commitment Therapy: contextualpsychology.org/act

Association for Behavioral and Cognitive Therapies: www.abct.org

Virtual reality treatments for PTSD: ptsd.about.com/od/treatment/a/VRexposure.htm

Healthy Lifestyle

Healthy eating:　　www.nutrition.gov

　　　　　　　　www.choosemyplate.gov

Fitness:　　　　　www.fitness.gov

Issue-Specific Support

Rape, Abuse and Incest National Network: www.rainn.org

Veterans: www.afterdeployment.org

The National Center for Victims of Crime: www.ncvc.org

National Domestic Violence Hotline: thehotline.org

Contacting a Therapist Trained in PTSD

Find a therapist: http://ptsd.about.com/od/ptsdbasics/tp/txproviders.htm

References

Acierno, R., M. A. Hernandez, A. B. Amstadter, H. S. Resnick, K. Steve, W. Muzzy, and D. G. Kilpatrick. 2010. Prevalence and Correlates of Emotional, Physical, Sexual, and Financial Abuse and Potential Neglect in the United States: The National Elder Mistreatment Study. *American Journal of Public Health* 100(2): 292–7.

Andreasen, N. C. 2010. Posttraumatic Stress Disorder: A History and a Critique. *Annals of the New York Academy of Sciences* 1208: 67–71.

Barlow, D. H. 2007. *Clinical Handbook of Psychological Disorders: A Step-by-Step Treatment Manual.* 4th ed. New York: Guilford Press.

Barlow, D. H., and M. G. Craske. 2006. *Mastery of Your Anxiety and Panic: Workbook.* New York: Oxford University Press.

Barlow, D. H., and V. M. Durand. 2011. *Abnormal Psychology: An Integrated Approach.* 6th ed. Belmont, CA: Wadsworth Publishing.

Becker, C. B., and C. Zayfert. 2001. Integrating DBT-Based Techniques and Concepts to Facilitate Exposure Treatment for PTSD. *Cognitive and Behavioral Practice* 8(2): 107–22.

Bertisch, S. M., C. C. Wee, R. S. Phillips, and E. P. McCarthy. 2009. Alternative Mind-Body Therapies Used by Adults with Medical Conditions. *Journal of Psychosomatic Research* 66(6): 511–19.

Bourne, E. J. 1995. *The Anxiety and Phobia Workbook.* Oakland, CA: New Harbinger.

Breiding, M. J., M. C. Black, and G. W. Ryan. 2008. Chronic Disease and Health Risk Behaviors Associated with Intimate Partner Violence—18 U.S. States/Territories, 2005. *Annals of Epidemiology* 18(7): 538–44.

Brewin, C. R., T. Dalgleish, and S. Joseph. 1996. A Dual Representation Theory of Posttraumatic Stress Disorder. *Psychological Review* 103(4): 670–86.

Burns, D. 1999. *Feeling Good: The New Mood Therapy*, revised and updated. New York: Harper.

Cahill, S. P., and E. B. Foa. 2007. Psychological Theories of PTSD. In *Handbook of PTSD: Science and Practice*, edited by M. Friedman, T. M. Keane, and P. A. Resick. New York: Guilford Press.

Chawla, N., and B. Ostafin. 2007. Experiential Avoidance as a Functional Dimensional Approach to Psychopathology: An Empirical Review. *Journal of Clinical Psychology* 63(9): 871–90.

Cukor, J., J. Spitalnick, J. Difede, A. Rizzo, and B. O. Rothbaum. 2009. Emerging Treatments for PTSD. *Clinical Psychology Review* 29(8): 715–26.

Dennis, M. F., A. M. Flood, V. Reynolds, G. Araujo, C. P. Clancy, J. C. Barefoot, and J. C. Beckham. 2009. Evaluation of Lifetime Trauma Exposure and Physical Health in Women with Posttraumatic Stress Disorder or Major Depressive Disorder. *Violence Against Women* 15(5): 618–27.

Descilo, T., A. Vedamurtachar, P. L. Gerbarg, D. Nagaraja, B. N. Gangadhar, B. Damodaran, B. Adelson, L. H. Braslow, S. Marcus, and R. P. Brown. 2010. Effects of a Yoga Breath Intervention Alone and in Combination with an Exposure Therapy for Post-Traumatic Stress Disorder and Depression in Survivors of the 2004 South-East Asia Tsunami. *Acta Psychiatrica Scandinavica* 121(4): 289–300.

Deykin, E. Y., T. M. Keane, D. Kaloupek, G. Fincke, J. Rothendler, M. Siegfried, and K. Creamer. 2001. Posttraumatic Stress Disorder and the Use of Health Services. *Psychosomatic Medicine* 63(5): 835–41.

Dutton, M. A., B. L. Green, S. I. Kaltman, D. M. Roesch, T. A. Zeffiro, and E. D. Krause. 2006. Intimate Partner Violence, PTSD, and Adverse Health Outcomes. *Journal of Interpersonal Violence* 21(7): 955–68.

Eifert, G., and J. P. Forsyth. 2005. *Acceptance and Commitment Therapy for Anxiety Disorders: A Practioner's Guide to Using Mindfulness, Acceptance, and Values-Based Behavior Change Strategies.* Oakland, CA: New Harbinger.

Elliott, D. M., D. S. Mok, and J. Briere. 2004. Adult Sexual Assault: Prevalence, Symptomatology, and Sex Differences in the General Population. *Journal of Traumatic Stress* 17(3): 203–11.

Felitti, V. J., R. F. Anda, D. Nordenberg, D. F. Williamson, A. M. Spitz, V. Edwards, M. P. Koss, and J. S. Marks. 1998. Relationship of Childhood Abuse and Household Dysfunction to Many of the Leading Causes of Death in Adults: The Adverse Childhood Experiences (ACE) Study. *American Journal of Preventive Medicine* 14(4): 245–58.

Foa, E. B., E. Hembree, and R. Olaslov. 2007. *Prolonged Exposure Therapy for PTSD: Emotional Processing of Traumatic Experiences: Therapist Guide.* New York: Oxford University Press.

Foa, E. B., T. M. Keane, and M. J. Friedman. 2000. *Effective Treatments for PTSD: Practice Guidelines from the International Society for Traumatic Stress Studies.* New York: Guilford Press.

Follette, V., K. A. Palm, and A. N. Pearson. 2006. Mindfulness and Trauma: Implications for Treatment. *Journal of Rational-Emotive and Cognitive-Behavior Therapy* 24(1): 45.

Friedman, M. J. 2003. *Post Traumatic Stress Disorder: The Latest Assessment and Treatment Strategies.* Kansas City, MO: Compact Clinicals.

Ganzel, B. L., J. J. Eckenrode, P. Kim, E. Wethington, E. Horowitz, and E. Temple. 2007. Salivary Cortisol Levels and Mood Vary by Lifetime Trauma Exposure in a Sample of Healthy Women. *Journal of Traumatic Stress* 20(5): 689–99.

Gray, M. J., Y. Schorr, W. Nash, L. Lebowitz, A. Amidon, A. Lansing, et al. 2012. Adaptive Disclosure: An Open Trial of a Novel Exposure-Based Intervention for Service Members with Combat-Related Psychological Stress Injuries. *Behavior Therapy* 43(2): 407–15.

Harned, M. S., S. C. Jackson, K. A. Comtois, and M. M. Linehan. 2010. Dialectical Behavior Therapy as a Precursor to PTSD Treatment for Suicidal and/or Self-Injuring Women with Borderline Personality Disorder. *Journal of Traumatic Stress* 23(4): 421–9.

Hayes, S. C., K. Strosahl, and K. G. Wilson. 1999. *Acceptance and Commitment Therapy: An Experiential Approach to Behavior Change.* New York: Guilford Press.

Hoffman, S., A. Sayer, and A. Fang. 2010. The Empirical Status of the New Wave of Cognitive Behavioral Therapy. *Psychiatric Clinics of North America* 33(3): 701–10.

Hynes, M., and B. L. Cardozo. 2000. Observations from the CDC: Sexual Violence against Refugee Women. *Journal of Women's Health and Gender-Based Medicine* 9(8): 819–23.

Janoff-Bulman, R. 2002. *Shattered Assumptions.* New York: Free Press.

Jones, E., and S. Wessely. 2006. *Shell Shock to PTSD: Military Psychiatry from 1900 to the Gulf War.* New York: Psychology Press.

Kabat-Zinn, J. 1994. *Wherever You Go, There You Are: Mindfulness Meditation in Everyday Life.* New York: Hyperion.

Kimerling, R., G. A. Clum, and J. Wolfe. 2000. Relationships among Trauma Exposure, Chronic Posttraumatic Stress Disorder Symptoms, and Self-Reported Health in Women: Replication and Extension. *Journal of Traumatic Stress* 13(1): 115

Kimerling, R., P. Ouimette, and J. Wolfe. 2002. *Gender and PTSD.* New York: Guilford Press.

Krakow, B., M. Hollifield, R. Schrader, M. Koss, D. Tandberg, J. Lauriello, L. McBride, et al. 2000. A Controlled Study of Imagery Rehearsal for Chronic Nightmares in Sexual Assault Survivors with PTSD: A Preliminary Report. *Journal of Traumatic Stress* 13(4): 589-609.

Lavie, P. 2001. Sleep Disturbances in the Wake of Traumatic Events. *New England Journal of Medicine* 345(25): 1825–32.

LeDoux, J. E. 1992. Brain Mechanisms of Emotion and Emotional Learning. *Current Opinion in Neurobiology* 2(2): 191–7.

Letourneau, E. J., M. Holmes, and J. Chasedunn-Roark. 1999. Gynecologic Health Consequences to Victims of Interpersonal Violence. *Women's Health Issues* 9(2): 115–20.

Linehan, M. M. 1993. *Cognitive Behavioral Treatment of Borderline Personality Disorder.* New York: Guilford Press.

Linehan, M. M., K. A. Comtois, A. M. Murray, M. Z. Brown, R. J. Gallop, H. L. Heard, K. E. Korslund, D. A. Tutek, S. K. Reynolds, and N. Lindenboim. 2006. Two-Year Randomized Controlled Trial and Follow-Up of Dialectical Behavior Therapy vs. Therapy by Experts for Suicidal Behaviors and Borderline Personality Disorder. *Archives of General Psychiatry* 63(7): 757–66.

Linley, P. A., and S. Joseph. 2004. Positive Change Following Trauma and Adversity: A Review. *Journal of Traumatic Stress* 17(1): 11–21.

Lutz, A., H. A. Slagter, J. D. Dunne, and R. J. Davidson. 2008. Attention Regulation and Monitoring in Meditation. *Trends in Cognitive Sciences* 12(4): 163–9.

Malta, L. S., K. E. Wyka, C. Giosan, N. Jayasinghe, and J. Difede. 2009. Numbing Symptoms as Predictors of Unremitting Posttraumatic Stress Disorder. *Journal of Anxiety Disorders* 23(2): 223–9.

Michenbaum, D. 2007. Stress Innoculation Training: A Preventative Treatment Approach. In *Principles and Practice of Stress Management*, edited by P. M. Lehrer, R. L. Woolfolk, and W. E. Sime. New York: Guilford Press.

Miller, W. R., and S. Rollnick. 2002. *Motivational Interviewing: Preparing People for Change.* 2nd ed. New York: Guilford Press.

Monson, C. M., P. P. Schnurr, P. A. Resick, M. J. Friedman, Y. Young-Xu, and S. P. Stevens. 2006. Cognitive Processing Therapy for Veterans with Military-Related Posttraumatic Stress Disorder. *Journal of Consulting and Clinical Psychology* 74(5): 898–907.

Ouimette, P., R. Cronkite, B. R. Henson, A. Prins, K. Gima, and R. H. Moos. 2004. Posttraumatic Stress Disorder and Health Status among Female and Male Medical Patients. *Journal of Traumatic Stress* 17(1): 1–9.

Perkonigg, A., T. Owashi, M. B. Stein, C. Kirschbaum, and H. U. Wittchen. 2009. Posttraumatic Stress Disorder and Obesity: Evidence for a Risk Association. *American Journal of Preventive Medicine* 36(1): 1–8.

Pilcher, J. J., and E. S. Ott. 1998. The Relationships between Sleep and Measures of Health and Well-Being in College Students: A Repeated Measures Approach. *Behavioral Medicine* 23(4): 170–8.

Powers, M. B., J. M. Halpern, M. P. Ferenschak, S. J. Gillihan, and E. B. Foa. 2010. A Meta-Analytic Review of Prolonged Exposure for Posttraumatic Stress Disorder. *Clinical Psychology Review* 30(6): 635.

Resick, P. A., and M. K. Schnicke. 1992. Cognitive Processing Therapy for Sexual Assault Victims. *Journal of Consulting and Clinical Psychology* 60(5): 748–56.

Roberts, A. L., S. E. Gilman, J. Breslau, N. Breslau, and K. C. Koenen. 2011. Race/Ethnic Differences in Exposure to Traumatic Events, Development of Post-Traumatic Stress Disorder, and Treatment-Seeking for Post-Traumatic Stress Disorder in the United States. *Psychological Medicine* 41(1): 71.

Roemer, L., and S. M. Orsillo. 2009. *Mindfulness- and Acceptance-Based Behavioral Therapies in Practice.* New York: Guilford Press.

Rollnick, S., W. R. Miller, and C. Butler. 2008. *Motivational Interviewing in Health Care: Helping Patients Change Behavior.* New York: Guilford Press.

Sadler, A. G., B. M. Booth, D. Nielson, and B. N. Doebbeling. 2000. Health-Related Consequences of Physical and Sexual Violence: Women in the Military. *Obstetrics and Gynecology* 96(3): 473–80.

Skinner, K. M., N. Kressin, S. Frayne, T. J. Tripp, C. S. Hankin, D. R. Miller, and L. M. Sullivan. 2000. The Prevalence of Military Sexual Assault among Female Veterans Administration Outpatients. *Journal of Interpersonal Violence* 15(3): 291–310.

Steenkamp, M. M., B. T. Litz, M. J. Gray, L. Lebowitz, W. Nash, L. Conoscenti, A. Amidon, and A. Lang. 2011. A Brief Exposure-Based Intervention for Service Members with PTSD. *Cognitive and Behavioral Practice* 18(1): 98–107.

Thompson, M. P., J. B. Kingree, and S. Desai. 2004. Gender Differences in Long-Term Health Consequences of Physical Abuse of Children: Data from a Nationally Representative Survey. *American Journal of Public Health* 94(4): 599–604.

Thompson, R. W., D. B. Arnkoff, and C. R. Glass. 2011. Conceptualizing Mindfulness and Acceptance as Components of Psychological Resilience to Trauma. *Trauma, Violence, and Abuse* 12(4): 220–35.

Tjaden, P., and N. Thoennes. 2000. *Extent, Nature, and Consequences of Intimate Partner Violence*. Research report. Washington, DC: U.S. Dept. of Justice, Office of Justice Programs, National Institute of Justice.

———. 1998. *Prevalence, Incidence, and Consequences of Violence against Women: Findings from the National Violence against Women Survey*. Research in brief. Washington, DC: U.S. Dept. of Justice, Office of Justice Programs, National Institute of Justice.

Ullman, S. E., and H. H. Filipas. 2001. Predictors of PTSD Symptom Severity and Social Reactions in Sexual Assault Victims. *Journal of Traumatic Stress* (14)2: 369–89.

Vujanovic, A. A., N. E. Youngwirth, K. A. Johnson, and M. J. Zvolensky. 2009. Mindfulness-Based Acceptance and Posttraumatic Stress Symptoms among Trauma-Exposed Adults without Axis I Psychopathology. *Journal of Anxiety Disorders* 23(2): 297–303.

Wagner, A. W., J. Wolfe, A. Rotnitsky, S. P. Proctor, and D. J. Erickson. 2000. An Investigation of the Impact of Posttraumatic Stress Disorder on Physical Health. *Journal of Traumatic Stress* 13(1): 41.

Wegner, D. M. 1987. Paradoxical Effect of Thought Suppression. *Journal of Personality and Social Psychology* 53(1): 5–13.

Zoellner, L. A., M. L. Goodwin, and E. B. Foa. 2000. PTSD Severity and Health Perceptions in Female Victims of Sexual Assault. *Journal of Traumatic Stress* 13(4): 635–49.

Sheela Raja, PhD, is a licensed clinical psychologist and assistant professor at the University of Illinois at Chicago. She completed internship and post-doctoral training at the National Center for Post-Traumatic Stress Disorder in Boston, MA, and has published numerous articles exploring the relationship between physical health and traumatic events. Raja has a passion for making evidence-based psychology accessible and is a frequent contributor to various print and national television media outlets.

Foreword writer **Susan M. Orsillo, PhD,** is professor of psychology at Suffolk University in Boston, and lives in the Boston area with her husband and two children. Orsillo has written and published extensively about mindfulness, anxiety, and psychotherapy, and has been involved in anxiety disorder research and treatment. She is the coauthor of the acclaimed book, *Mindfulness and Acceptance-Based Behavioral Therapies in Practice,* as well as *The Mindful Way through Anxiety.*

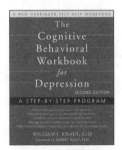

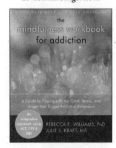